READ THIS WHEN THINGS FALL APART

PRAISE FOR: *READ THIS WHEN THINGS FALL APART*

"What a gift! We all need these letters, not just in times of crisis or defeat. It is the only book you'll hold that will hold you, free you, permit you to fail, rest, retreat, grieve, live, laugh, fight, and heal—to be human. This book must never go out of print." —**Robin D. G. Kelley, author of *Freedom Dreams: The Black Radical Imagination***

"*Read this When Things Fall Apart* is a balm of these dark times. This is the book I wish I'd had as a young organizer. It is a necessary text that sent me through the full kaleidoscope of emotions—spanning rage, laughter, and sadness—but more importantly, helped ground me in times of crisis and unrelenting brutality." —**Robyn Maynard, co-author of *Rehearsals for Living***

"If you need an antidote to despair, this book is for you. It's a repository of fortifying collective wisdom, a tonic for our troubled times. The letters Kelly Hayes has collected offer vital insights amid the darkness, shrewd strategic advice for aspiring change-makers, and a reminder none of us are in the fight alone." —**Astra Taylor, co-author of *Solidarity: The Past, Present, and Future of a World-Changing Idea***

"For years I've had a saying: resist the pleasures of doom. It can feel perversely good to tell ourselves that the situation is so bad we simply can't do anything, to throw up our hands and give up. This book is an antidote to the pleasures of doom—it offers the deeper, more sustaining pleasure of solidarity, in beautiful specificity, from committed organizers in a variety of movements. They have felt despair, stared into the void of defeat, and they share concrete advice about the ways we can keep going when all feels hopeless. This book is a profound act of care." —**Sarah Jaffe, author of *From the Ashes: Grief and Revolution in a World on Fire***

"*Read this When Things Fall Apart: Letters to Activists in Crisis* is a signpost for activists who feel unsettled about themselves and the future. The contributors offer their truths and wisdom with raw vulnerability. *Read this When Things Fall Apart* is a resource for anyone who believes hope will guide us through the darkest of times." —**Alice Wong, editor of *Disability Intimacy: Essays on Love, Care, and Desire***

"These letters are like seeds in a pomegranate—gorgeous gems full of nourishment, nestled together, shaped by one another, juicy, sweet and alive. The intimacy and urgency of these wise messages, written by people who have given so much to our movements and seen so much, is just what we need right now, in harrowing times, to help new people cross the threshold to collective action and to bolster the spirits of all who continue to press on, against difficult odds. I cannot wait to give this book to my students and the people I've been working with for decades. We all need what is in here." —**Dean Spade, author of *Mutual Aid: Building Solidarity During This Crisis (and the Next)***

"These letters of love have emerged from Kelly's wide community of friends, organizers and kindred spirits. They represent the best of our humanity, teaching us what we need to know, as we struggle to be healthy, happy and free." —**Lisa Fithian, author of *Shut It Down: Stories from a Fierce, Loving Resistance***

"A glorious and generous offering, right on time for new and seasoned organizers alike. I picked it up in a moment of flagging hope and put it down feeling profoundly fortified in the unshakeable truth that courage is collective—and creative—and that building and strengthening communities of care and resistance is our most critical assignment in this moment. A collection of poignant reminders that we can never give up on ourselves, each other, or the endless possibilities for liberatory futures that lie in uncertainty and beautiful struggle." —**Andrea J. Ritchie, author of *Practicing New Worlds: Abolition and Emergent Strategies***

"In this time of monsters burying us in grief and despair, this extraordinary collection is a steady hand with advice, analysis and affirmation. Each generous and generative letter centers our love for ourselves and our people as methodology. This book is a compelling reminder that we need each other as comrades and community, that we all have gifts to contribute to movements, and that—through uncertainty and one million experiments—we will win." —**Harsha Walia, author of *Border and Rule: Global Migration, Capitalism, and the Rise of Racist Nationalism***

READ THIS WHEN THINGS FALL APART

Letters to Activists in Crisis

Edited by Kelly Hayes

AK PRESS

Read This When Things Fall Apart: Letters to Activists in Crisis
© 2025 Edited by Kelly Hayes
All essays © 2025 by their respective authors
This edition © 2025 AK Press

ISBN 978-1-84935-584-1
E-ISBN: 978-1-84935-585-8
Audiobook: 978-1-84935-652-7

LCCN: 2025937201

AK Press
370 Ryan Avenue #100
Chico, CA 95973
USA
www.akpress.org
akpress@akpress.org

AK Press
33 Tower Street
Edinburgh
Scotland EH6 7BN
www.akuk.com
akuk@akpress.org

Please contact us to request the latest AK Press distribution catalog, which features books, pamphlets, zines, and stylish apparel published and/or distributed by AK Press. Alternatively, visit our websites for the complete catalog, latest news, and secure ordering.

Cover illustration and titling by Olly Costello
Printed in the United States of America on acid-free paper

For all of the activists, organizers, movement artists, healers, water protectors, land defenders, mutual aid workers, truth tellers, and freedom fighters who have refused to give up—or who gave up, but came back.

Letter Directory

Read This . . .

Introduction: If You Feel Like You're Falling
Kelly Hayes 1

If You're New and Trying to Find Your Way
Mariame Kaba 9

If You're Witnessing the Unthinkable
Eman Abdelhadi 13

If You're Losing and Discouraged
Micah Herskind 23

If Someone You Loved Has Killed Themself or Wants to,
and Maybe You Want to Too but You Also Want to Survive
Leah Lakshmi Piepzna-Samarasinha 33

If You Are Struggling with Your Mental Health
Aaron Goggans 51

If You Are Organizing Outside the Law
Brit "Red" Schulte 63

If You've Been Assaulted (I Believe You)
Leanne Betasamosake Simpson 69

If You're a Parent Feeling Isolated
Atena Danner 73

If You Are Panicking About Collapse
Chris Begley 89

If You Want to Defeat Fascism
Shane Burley 95

If You Are Overwhelmed by Attacks on
Reproductive Autonomy
Renee Bracey Sherman 111

If Injustice Has Alienated You from Your Community
Maya Schenwar 117

If You Are a Discouraged Incarcerated Organizer
Stevie Wilson 127

If You Are Heartbroken
Ashon Crawley 133

If You Want to Fight Big Tech
Brian Merchant 139

If You're Hurting and Want to Find Your People
Ash Williams 145

If You're Disabled and Trying to Figure Things Out
Leah Lakshmi Piepzna-Samarasinha and Jane Shi 153

If You Are Fighting Deportations and You're Afraid
or Discouraged
Aly Wane 167

If You Are Struggling With Grief
Tanuja Devi Jagernauth 175

Conclusion: If You're Wounded and Want to Quit
Kelly Hayes 187

Relating to the Origin
Atena Danner 197

Acknowledgments 201

READ THIS
THIS
WHEN THINGS FALL APART

Introduction
Read This If You Feel Like You're Falling

Kelly Hayes

Dear sibling in struggle,

When I was a child, I had nightmares about falling. There were no sights, no sounds, nothing to grab onto, and nowhere to land: just a pitch-black void and the sensation of plummeting. Like any child, I also had bad dreams about monsters and real-world scenarios, but nothing frightened me as much as those spiraling descents into the unknown. Decades later, I can recall the sensation with perfect clarity, and sometimes, I feel it when I'm wide awake.

We live in daunting times. Wildfires and hurricanes are stripping away the worlds we knew, while soaring temperatures are making large swaths of land unlivable. Big Tech—an industry bent on devouring every other industry—is now devouring governments as well. Our phones and laptops deliver endless reels of atrocity, fueling outrage and action while also scarring our psyches and our souls. From genocidal violence to the rise of authoritarianism, we are forever bearing witness, but the system has deemed our testimony irrelevant. In this era of smash-and-grab politics, ecosystems and futures are dismantled like stolen cars and sold for parts. To survive and cultivate meaning, amid so much collapse, we have to change everything—and we are going to need each other.

I am an organizer. I have a moral and political commitment to collective action, and to efforts to change and perhaps even save our world. Across the course of that work, which spans many years, movements, and battles lost and won, I have encountered moments of abject grief, profound loss, and mind-numbing confusion. I have experienced a spectrum of crises, from heartbreak and betrayal to the need to reckon with my own mistakes. Sometimes, the way forward is clear, even if that path is plagued with difficulty. At other times, I've found myself adrift in uncharted territory—grappling with a question, a feeling, or a trauma that no one around me seems to understand.

If you are navigating such waters, this book was written for you, with love and care, by a group of activists, organizers, and co-strugglers who want to hold you in this moment. We know that you are experiencing setbacks, heartbreaks, disappointments, and losses, because these crises have happened before and will happen again. Our movements are imperfect, because people are imperfect. Our good intentions do not exempt us from enacting or experiencing harm. We also know that the support and encouragement we need to face the everyday realities of organizing—such as what it feels like to be a newcomer, or to grapple with threats to our safety and freedom—aren't always available to us. Even when our co-strugglers are doing their best to hold us up, we may need to hear from someone else—an empathetic voice of experience that simply isn't in the room, or, perhaps, isn't there at 2:00 a.m. when our minds are racing and we cannot sleep. We wrote this book with those moments in mind, to provide you with a bundle of letters, written to friends and co-strugglers we haven't met yet, to offer you some accompaniment, advice, and analysis about movement work, relationship building, and the work of collective survival.

For me, learning to navigate my own trauma responses, and how to confront situations where I feel powerless, or have no idea what to do, has been a years-long process. Like many people, I have a low tolerance for uncertainty. I take comfort in feeling like I know what to do, even when I know it won't be easy. Justice work has forced me to confront the reality that uncertainty is where possibility resides. To sustain this work, we must imagine a world beyond what we've been told is inevitable, beyond what probable trends dictate—and there is no certainty in that experiment. So I must move through that realm of uncertainty, with all of its unwanted surprises, tragic twists, and possibilities.

Sometimes, when my efforts falter and human ugliness swells, I feel like a child spiraling in the dark. I have been rescued, amid many spirals, by the voices and outstretched hands of friends and co-strugglers—people whose insights helped ground me so that my life and work could go on. Some of the people who have offered that kind of help and guidance are featured in this book.

Community is essential, and this book is no substitute for the political homes, peace circles, organizations, affinity groups, and mutual aid projects that you will join in your efforts to remake the world. Finding your people is what makes meaningful change possible, at the community level and in the larger world. Having a community, and being accountable to that community, has shaped my life, my character, and my sense of purpose. However, there are moments when the fact that I have found my people simply isn't enough. There are moments so heavy and full of gut-wrenching disappointment that I don't know what to do with it all. I have found a number of tools, resources, and practices—such as therapy, writing and reading poetry, and engaging with nature—that often help me find my way. It is my sincerest hope that the letters in this book will serve as tools and resources to which you can turn in such moments.

This book is not an organizing handbook. It is a humble, personal offering grounded in an awareness that there are some moments, on all fronts of struggle, when, despite all of our best efforts, things fall apart. At such times, we sometimes need a kind, thoughtful voice amid the chaos or an outstretched hand to reach for.

We wrote these pages for you, a beleaguered human being who wants to change (or even save) the world; to tell you that you are not alone. We have been where many of you are, and we have continued on. We want to tell you how we have managed to move forward, and what keeps us moving, in the hopes that our words might help you do the same.

To refuse to give up is stubborn, creative, collective work. When we lose hard-fought battles, or beloved co-strugglers, the cruelties of capitalism and empire are compounded. Sometimes, the transformations we model are ripped apart before our eyes, as encampments are raided and community projects are destroyed. Sometimes, the social progress we've won is clawed back by our oppressors. Sometimes, we are left grieving amid the embers and echoes of collapsed movements, as injustice rages on.

Like my book with Mariame Kaba, *Let This Radicalize You*, which contains a lot of practical advice about organizing, this book began as a zine. Some friends and I wanted to collect letters to which activists in crisis could turn during the tumultuous years ahead. Many of us have engaged with letter writing as a form of political action. Some of us write letters to incarcerated co-strugglers, defying the culture of separation and forgetting that prisons impose upon us. During my earliest activist efforts, most people didn't have email addresses, and there were no online petitions. Recruiting someone to participate in a campaign often involved asking them to write a letter. In addition to being steeped in important political traditions—from anti-slavery organizing to the labor movement and beyond—letters are also a departure from the norms of the information and attention economy, where communication is often stunted and impersonal. Letter writing, as a practice, can help us hold each other in our humanity and think in less on-line terms. My sister, for example, will sometimes write me letters in Menominee, our Native language. Only about a dozen people speak Menominee fluently, most of them elders. My sister is studying our language, as a means of embracing our culture and endeavoring to sustain it. Her letters challenge me to look up the words she is using, so that I, too, might learn more of our language, while also understanding her better. Letters can represent a shared journey.

As the letters featured here accumulated, it became clear that this project was not the compact effort we had originally imagined. It was a book. Given this was a labor of love, which began with a group of friends and a simple idea, there are many issues and perspectives that are not represented here. We acknowledge those limitations, but we believe the web of experience and insight you will find in these pages is worth sharing.

While I haven't previously worked closely with everyone featured in this book, this effort is largely the product of relationships. I met Ash Williams—who wrote a letter for this book about reproductive justice and finding your people—in a warehouse about a decade ago, when I was leading a direct action training. Ash would soon ask me to be his mentor in direct action. Years later, Ash would, in turn, mentor me as I set out to become an abortion doula. Tanuja Jagernauth, whose letter in this book discusses the navigation of grief, co-organized with me in the early days of the pandemic when we were part of the Mutual Aid Mourning and Healing Project, which connected grieving people with peer support and helped organize online memorials. Red Schulte's letter about harm reduction and organizing outside the law is deeply personal to me, as Red has long been one of my own beloved partners in crime. Red and I have taken risks, endured losses, and helped empty cages together, and their tenacity and hard-won wisdom are offered here in loving, personal terms. I also treasure my dear friend Eman Abdelhadi, whose letter about bearing witness to atrocity, and the genocide of her people, is one of the most profound and beautiful interventions in this book. My co-struggler Stevie Wilson, a movement educator and prison organizer, brought the crucial tradition of corresponding with incarcerated comrades to this book, and I couldn't be more grateful for him or his insights. By and large, I think of this book as something I made for you with my friends, and I hope it is a gift accepted in that spirit.

Each of the letters in this book is an effort to reach you, a co-struggler we probably haven't met yet, as you grapple with conflicts, tragedies, and questions with which we have been confronted in our work. Some of these letters may refer to situations you have never experienced, and some may feel as though they were written just for you. My advice is to read each of them, including those you cannot immediately relate to. Life is unpredictable, and discussions that do not feel relevant right now could become essential in time. More importantly, the insights shared in each letter may apply to some aspect of your own struggles, or to the struggles of those around you, even if that insight was born of circumstances you have never experienced. Perhaps these pages will inspire you to write your own letter, and to share it with someone who needs your experience, strength, and hope.

When I was so wrapped up in the urgency of a crisis that I was ready to work myself to death (perhaps literally), Tanuja reminded me that our work is collective, and that I must preserve my well-being. When I have been overwhelmed by the march of authoritarianism and fascistic politics, my friend Shane Burley has helped me formulate an analysis of the moment, and a sense of strategy about how to meet it. When I have been aching from a harsh defeat, or a personal loss, the words of Aly Wane, Mariame Kaba, and Maya Schenwar have helped lift me out of despair. I hope that their offerings, and the many other perspectives offered in this text, provide you with some of the understanding and support you need to do whatever the next right thing might be in your life and in your work. More than anything, my friends and I wanted to make something that you could carry with you, as you face the heartbreaks, setbacks, and confounding questions that emerge when we choose to fight, in collectivity, in the hopes of saving ourselves and each other.

I know that work of justice and changemaking will continue. It always has. My concern, as I write these words, is that you are able to stay with us in this struggle, as we fight for what could be. There are no fairytale endings and no shortcuts. What we have is each other and our will to remake the world. I cannot tell you it will be enough, because I do not know what the future holds.

However, I can tell you that we and the world are worth fighting for, and that there is love, hope, and purpose to be found in the pursuit of justice, and in the work of collective survival. Yes, there is joy in struggle, even as the world falls down. There is dancing amid the destruction.

In solidarity,
Kelly Hayes

Read This if You're New and Trying to Find Your Way
Mariame Kaba

Dear Young Organizer/Activist,

    I'm writing this letter during deeply unsettling and troubled times. We are living through extremely turbulent and horrific events, including several genocides, acute climate change, many wars, growing criminalization, increasing inequality, the rise of fascism, and much more. It feels like the world is on fire because it is.

    As an activist and organizer, you are sometimes called upon to be not just a firefighter but to rebuild in a new and better way. We have to help people understand what is (the current, shared reality), we must collectively imagine what can be (a future possibility), and we have to diligently labor for what must be (organizing to sustain life/livingness and for liberation).

    These days, people around me are using the word "despair" with regularity. Perhaps you are experiencing the same. Given the stakes, I can understand being despairing. Yet I'm with Audre Lorde, who wrote that "despair is a tool of our enemies." Why do I believe this? Because despair has a way of distorting, it often pairs well with cynicism, which I see as a way of being that contracts what's possible rather than expanding possibilities. Rather than being enabling, I have experienced it as corrosive. Are cynical people builders? I haven't experienced them as such. I'm with Max Horkheimer, the philosopher who argued that cynicism is "another mode of conformity." I heard writer Maria Popova say in a podcast interview that she lives in "defiance of despair." This resonated with me. It's my experience that taking positive collective action can crowd out despair. It offers a little bit of light and helps you to perceive yourself and your community more clearly.

I'm regularly asked about hope. I've said that for me hope is a discipline, a practice that I engage in daily (and on some days hourly). Sometimes people say to me that hope is a disposition, and that you either have it or you don't. I vehemently disagree.

Some people seem to think of hope as "wishful thinking." For me, it's not that at all. Rather, because I don't know how things will turn out, I choose to take action in the direction that I want to influence. I devote my efforts to making what I want to happen *actually happen*. Nothing can happen if we don't take action. As Annie Dillard writes: "How we spend our days is, of course, how we spend our lives. What we do with this hour, and that one, is what we are doing." I would add that how you do anything is how you do everything.

Action is a practice of hope. Put another way, hope is generated through action. "Doing" allows us to derive experience and meaning—it is through doing that we experience feeling. I'm interested in a robust and active hope, the kind of hope that has dirty and calloused hands.

So I wake up every single day and decide to practice hope. The reason I do so is that this is something that falls solely under my control. I can't control social forces, but I can choose to practice hope by taking my own considered daily actions. I have learned a lot from Joanna Macy's concept of active hope. For Macy, active hope doesn't require optimism. We can cultivate it no matter how we are feeling (for example, you can still cultivate hope while you grieve, while you feel despondent, and so on). Hope makes room for itself, beside every emotion. Hope is not the belief that everything will turn out well—that's optimism, and I'm not an optimist.

I'm also interested in how Joan Halifax invites us to lean into uncertainty and the unknown as we practice what she calls wise hope. We are always going to be surprised in good and bad directions. That grounds me. I know things change all the time, even though I never know what direction that change will take.

I don't know how things will turn out, but I am committed to something other than this—the current structure and state of this world. We can live differently. I don't think we have to live the way we currently do. I think something else is possible. The social theorist Henri Giroux writes that "hope expands the space of the possible and becomes a way of recognizing and naming the incomplete nature of the present." So I invite you, young organizer, to embrace uncertainty as a terrain of glorious possibility. Let this uncertainty ground you rather than make you fearful.

I know that hope isn't something everyone embraces, and I respect this. I usually tell my loved ones who adamantly reject it that it's okay if they give up hope, so long as they don't give up trying. Don't give up on taking action. Our present actions matter, even though we do not know how the future will turn out. I'm with Grace Lee Boggs, who said: "We never know how our small activities will affect others through the invisible fabric of our connectedness. In this exquisitely connected world, it's never a question of critical mass. It's always about critical connections."

Every time we choose constructive action, it builds toward the possibility of freedom and liberation.

So as long as I am alive, I'm going to keep trying every day. That's my commitment. Every morning that I have breath, I stay rooted in possibility and I choose to act. And I remember that doing so doesn't preclude feeling burdened or needing relief.

There's a poem by Brendan Kennelly that I appreciate titled "Begin," and I love this part in particular because for me, it speaks to hope as a discipline:

> Though we live in a world that dreams of ending
> that always seems about to give in
> something that will not acknowledge conclusion
> insists that we forever begin

So, young organizer, make space in your life to begin again every single day. Be astonished at mundane things in your world. Build positive actions into the fabric of your life. As Emily Raboteau has said, the "future is not foreclosed." We'll get through this together. That's a promise.

In peace,
Mariame

Mariame Kaba is the cofounder and co-lead of Interrupting Criminalization with fellow organizer Andrea J. Ritchie. Kaba is the author of the *New York Times* Best Seller *We Do This 'Til We Free Us: Abolitionist Organizing and Transforming Justice* (Haymarket Books, 2021), among several other titles that offer support and tools for repair, transformation, and moving toward a future without incarceration and policing.

Read This if You're Witnessing the Unthinkable
Eman Abdelhadi

Habibi,

    I write this to you from the comfort of a heated home on a quiet street, where no bombs are likely to fall, where water flows from taps and refrigerators hum with plentitude. Perhaps you are reading this from a similar home, where the sky does not threaten to fall. And yet, perhaps, like me, you have been glued to a screen that brings you death and destruction, and the images from your phone screen feel more real than the images outside your window.

    I am writing in February 2024, in the fifth month of the genocide in Gaza.

    Perhaps, like me, you are acutely and increasingly aware that you are leading a life stolen from the clutches of fate; that your survival is an accident of time and place. Perhaps, like me, you are struggling to understand the cruelty of luck. People that look like you and me belong where water is scarce, where food trucks squeeze through borders, where no shelter can live up to its name. Perhaps, like me, you wonder what you are doing here, why you are not living, and indeed dying, among your people.

    Perhaps you exit your home to a sea of blank white faces. You observe them as though you have somehow slipped into a parallel universe, invisible and confused. How could the world be both this and that? Here and there? There, homes turn into rubble, hospitals collapse onto their desperate patients, and mass graves fill with tiny bodies. People who could have been your siblings, your parents, your children—people who could have been you—are slaughtered or left to die of hunger and disease. Here, McMansions. Seven-dollar lattes. Thousand-dollar concert tickets. There, oblivion. Here, the oblivious.

You may be asking yourself, Am I dead and walking among the living? Or am I alive and walking among the dead?

I cannot excuse or even make sense of a society where speaking up against a genocide can mean losing your job, your housing, or even your life. We live among people to whom our lives are entirely dispensable. I do not know how to make that okay. Frankly, I do not care to.

But here we are in the heart of empire, at the end of the world. We cannot cede the future. So we have to figure out how to live and how to fight through the madness and the guilt of surviving when so many of our people have not. I have no answers, but I have strategies. I am writing to tell you how I have managed to stay alive and in struggle, in hopes some of this helps you stay and fight too.

Over the past four months, I have become—like many other Palestinians—a pared-down version of myself. I have expanded my movement work in a moment of immense trauma and grief, and thus have had to become ruthlessly protective of my time and energy. Reflecting on what has sustained me and my work, three pillars emerge: action, community, and imagination. I will elaborate on each of these and how they have inspired and reoriented my daily life.

Action

Since October 2023, I have watched hundreds of people turn into activists overnight—applying every possible skill and resource toward ending the genocide. The writers have written. The speakers have spoken. The organizers have organized. But so much more has happened behind the scenes. An herbalist friend started sending remedy gift baskets to organizers in her life, things to calm their nerves and help them ground themselves as they took on the work of mobilizing their communities. Another friend offered free massages. A tattoo artist was raffling tattoos to anyone donating to Palestine Legal. Everyone has something to offer. Use every skill you have, every resource you have for liberation. Activate the people around you to do the same.

Yes, go to protests, attend events, join meetings, but I am also urging you to transform whatever skills you already have into service for the movement. I am also suggesting that movement work can happen outside those official activist spaces and can be integrated into your day-to-day life. One dear friend and comrade called elected officials every day over coffee; another started a daily Zoom conference call for folks to do a quick phone bank after work. A third friend started skipping one coffee a day and sent the money she saved to activist bail funds. These strategies can outlive emergency moments like this one.

While you should generally try to focus on actions that maximize your unique skill sets, when your energy is waning it may be time to shift course. A few weeks into the genocide, I realized I had very little time to engage in actions that nourished and sustained me. I was mostly writing and editing statements, fielding press calls, and attending an endless stream of meetings. That work was important, but it was depleting. I had very little to hold me as I watched Israel slaughter thousands upon thousands in Gaza. I found myself sleeping and crying more and more, struggling to function, entering a depressive state.

Then came the National March on Washington in November 2023. On the airplane with me were several people clearly on their way to the march. I chatted with a woman headed there with her son, his Palestine necklace identifying them just as my keffiyeh identified me. I asked if they were with a particular group, and she replied, "No. We're just tired of watching."

I arrived in a DC transformed by the hundreds of thousands there to attend the march. Everywhere we walked that weekend, Palestine was present. Posters for the march lined the streets, and keffiyehs lined the streets. We marched while singing and chanting, imagining our liberated homeland and reveling in the sweet solidarity of having found each other. The march did not need me; I needed the march.

As a sociologist, I often teach a concept called collective effervescence. It is the warm, fuzzy feeling of being part of a group. It is the high you might get at a concert or at a protest, and it plays an essential part in giving us a sense of belonging and solidarity. When your energy is waning, prioritize actions that will inspire that feeling of collective effervescence. When I returned to Chicago, it was with a new well of energy and enthusiasm that would last me many more weeks.

Finally, limit your time on social media. As the world's elites have been determined to turn us away from the travesties happening in Gaza, many of us have rightly felt we had to bear witness to the death and destruction our tax dollars are funding. Bearing witness has been crucial. However, videos and photos of the dead and dying expose us to an avalanche of trauma that can quickly become debilitating. We have had to find a balance between meeting our duty to bear witness and taking enough breaks to continue to be effective as organizers and activists. That balance is particularly hard to find because many of us receive our news primarily from social media, which is full of horrifying images and videos but is not always as replete with information.

I have found it helpful to read trusted news sources rather than scroll through Instagram. While I was glued to the news for the first two weeks or so, I then transitioned to reading it two to three times a day rather than plugging in continuously. I spent more time on Twitter (recently renamed X), which served me updates primarily as text rather than image. I also found it helpful to set limits on my screen time, particularly applications that prioritize video and photo content. Our job as survivors is to—in the oft-used phrase—fight like hell for the living. Trauma, even consumed through a screen, can put you into a state of shock. When you are in shock, you are not in fighting shape.

Community and Care

Find your people, and create networks of support, care, and trust. Since October, my social circle has both expanded and contracted. I have shed any relationships where the simple fact of the genocide is under question. I realized I could not preserve my energy for the work if I had to convince a friend or colleague of my humanity. In a moment where the global ruling class, with its media and education apparatus, has been gaslighting Palestinians, I could still choose not to allow gaslighting in my personal life.

I also minimized relationships with people whose politics move them only to theory and not action, or who prioritize critique over engagement. In *Let This Radicalize You* by Mariame Kaba and Kelly Hayes—Kaba shares a story of critiquing a movement space, only to have an elder ask, "What have you built?" Surround yourself with people who spend more time building than tearing down. The naysayers, the what-about-ers, the armchair commentators, the more-radical-than-thou movement cannabilizers—they have all had to go. I love many of those people, and I will return to tending to those relationships when the crisis phase of this moment has passed. However, for now, I have maintained active relationships only with those who understand that action is imperative and that movements require that we fight on multiple fronts. We have to understand that everything we do is both important and not enough.

Let people support you. Maybe you spend your time organizing direct actions but someone in your life cannot do that type of work. Perhaps they cannot risk arrest, because of an immigration case, care obligations, or a disability. They offer to send you food. Say yes. The meal they make you is a contribution to the direct actions you are planning. Feminist theory teaches us that the labor of social reproduction—cooking, cleaning, childcare, and all of the other work necessary to sustain ourselves as people and as communities—is an essential part of all productive labor in society. Capitalism has tried to render that work invisible, but we know better. Contributing to our movements are not just the speechmakers and action-planners but also those who feed and clothe us—near and far.

Take care of someone else. Sandi Hilal, a Palestinian artist, has long argued that hosting is a sacred right that the displaced lose upon losing their homes. Along with her creative partner, architect Alessandro Petti, she has installed tent-shaped concrete shelters in refugee camps in Palestine, Lebanon, and elsewhere. They represent the permanence of displacement, but they also become communal spaces where refugees can take on the role of hosts. Hilal and Petti's work reminds us that our humanity is reinforced not just by receiving care but by giving it.

In these past four months, I have felt most grounded in moments where I had to step out of my own pain to care for another person. Running an errand for a friend, cooking for my partner, holding a sobbing comrade as they processed loss—these moments have reminded me that I am capable, that I am an important member of a network of care. In other words, they have told me that my existence matters for those that I love.

Imagination

Over the last few months, the movement for Palestinian liberation in the United States has met the brief. We have altered public opinion of Israel and its apartheid regime in ways none of us thought imaginable. At the time of writing this, 60 percent of Americans and 80 percent of Democrats support a permanent ceasefire. Younger generations are overwhelmingly critical of Israel and supportive of the Palestinian struggle for freedom and self-determination. We have placed enormous pressure on both government and civil society institutions to push for accountability for Israel's crimes.

Yet, we have been ignored, and little has changed for Palestinians on the ground in response to our efforts. I have been jarred by the whiplash between being a part of a growing, vibrant social movement and watching the killing continue unabated. It is easy to feel helpless. We live in a class dictatorship thinly disguised as a democracy. Our speech is not free, and the level of surveillance and repression by the state and its parallel institutions has been astounding. Even in our colleges and universities—institutions whose primary missions are the spread of knowledge and free inquiry—the will of donors has overruled the edicts of open discourse and student needs.

It is hard to imagine a way out of this. And it is not just Palestine. We live on a planet we are actively destroying, and the climate crisis has made every year feel more apocalyptic than the one before. Like me, you probably have friends who say they cannot have children under these conditions, that they do not want to bring humans into the end of humanity. An artist I am close to describes their job as being a doula for humanity as we approach extinction.

I reject this vision of the future, and I lament that the ruling class has robbed many of us even of our ability to imagine a world outside their grasp.

We have to imagine the world we are trying to win.

In 2022, my best friend M. E. O'Brien and I published a speculative fiction novel, *Everything for Everyone: An Oral History of the New York Commune, 2052–2072*, that foretells a global revolution where capitalism and the nation-state fall, giving way to a more equitable and free future. Neither of us is a novelist, and we published with a small leftist press that we knew would be amenable to our communist tendencies. We were both delighted and surprised by the warm reception the novel met.

I am proud of our novel, but I think it did well primarily because it is of this moment, a moment where so many are desperate to reclaim their imaginations. But we need not go far into the future to imagine a world that is ruled not by profit but by collective action and common good.

In talks and interviews across the country, M. E. and I have been asked about our inspiration for imagining this world that is seemingly so different from our own. We have invariably referred to the real-life social movements we have participated in or witnessed: watching protest kitchen and medic tents emerge in Tahrir Square or Zuccotti Park; watching people converge on Standing Rock to reassert Indigenous claims to the land; watching mutual aid resuscitate communities after climate-induced catastrophes; watching young people set fire to police stations and cars in response to the murder of George Floyd. Each of these moments and dozens more have been acts of speculative fiction, acts of imagination that reorganized our social world away from profit and toward liberation.

I repeat: we have to imagine the world we are trying to win, for ourselves and for our small social worlds. We can imagine it in our day-to-day lives as movement practitioners, in the ways we treat each other and our communities. How would we treat each other if we weren't competing over scarce resources? How would we treat our bodies if we did not have to slave over wages? How would we treat our environment or our possessions if we were not ruled by cheap consumerism? Which of these ethos could we bring to our lives today?

For our movements, we must also imagine the world we are trying to win. What would it take for Palestine to be free—truly free? What would a free Palestine look like? Smell like? Feel like? On a trip to Palestine in 2016, I sat in a coffee shop with other activists and imagined a world where we could drive from Jerusalem to Gaza for a picnic by the sea. That journey, one that should take only a couple of hours, is currently impossible, but it is not unimaginable. I have to believe that one day I will take that drive. If I do not, my children will. If not them, their children. I believe, I believe that we will win. I invite you to believe with me.

Fi amanillah,
Eman Abdelhadi

Eman Abdelhadi (she/they) is an organizer, writer, and scholar based in Chicago. She is coauthor of the revolutionary sci-fi novel *Everything for Everyone: An Oral History of the New York Commune, 2052–2072* (Common Notions, 2022). Abdelhadi is a sociologist and assistant professor at the University of Chicago, where her research focuses on migration, gender, and Muslim communities. She cofounded the Salon Kawakib collective, and she organizes with Faculty and Staff for Justice in Palestine.

Read This if You're Losing and Discouraged
Micah Herskind

Dear Friend,
 I'm writing to you at the end of 2024. Things feel really horrible. The walls seem to be closing in. The fascist creep, police terror, and imperialist wars that we witness daily are deeply bipartisan ventures, cheered on with bloodlust from both sides of the aisle. Donald Trump was just elected, again, and the outgoing president spent the past year aiding, abetting, and facilitating genocide.
 Truthfully, things have felt bad for a while. The year 2023 began with the murder of Tortuguita, a queer Indigenous Venezuelan forest defender who was living in Atlanta's Weelaunee Forest to protect it against destruction and the creation of a sprawling police militarization facility known as Cop City. The year ended with a genocidal campaign against Palestinians, backed by the full force of the US government. Across these atrocities, mainstream media has served as a megaphone for state and corporate interests, painting victims as aggressors and resistors as terrorists. As people have risen up against environmental devastation, police expansion, and genocide, the state has aggressively deployed the tools of policing, prosecution, and caging in attempts to crush movements and ruin lives. Currently, sixty-one Stop Cop City activists are facing baseless conspiracy charges under the Racketeer Influenced and Corrupt Organizations (RICO) Act, and police across the world have conducted mass arrests of those protesting Israel's genocide of Palestinians.

I know you're struggling. I am too. Honestly, I'd be skeptical of anyone who is not struggling in some way right now. And as a relatively young organizer, I cannot say with certainty that things will end up okay. Like me, you've probably chanted, "When we fight, we win!" But for as many times as I've repeated this phrase, unfortunately it's not always true. We've fought for a lot of things and suffered lots of demoralizing losses. In this moment, when the defeats feel too discouraging, I cannot tell you that fighting will always lead to a win.

But I can tell you about the ways that I have seen people fight for a better world in the face of horrible odds, and why that fight has been worth it every time—even when we've lost. I can tell you why I think it matters that time and again, there are people who say no to the status quo, and who fight for a different future. I can tell you why I think it's worth it for you to keep fighting, despite the despair.

I want to tell you about the struggle to Stop Cop City, a movement that has fought since early 2021 to stop the destruction of over 380 acres of the Weelaunee Forest, a stretch of land in a majority-Black area of Southeast Atlanta that has been called one of the four "lungs" of the city. The land is under threat from a powerful coalition of state and corporate actors, who publicly released plans in spring of 2021 to destroy the forest and turn it into a massive urban-warfare training center for police.

There are many stories that could be told about this struggle: stories of the decentralized movement's militant tactics, such as sabotage of construction machinery and courageous land defense; stories of deep relationship-building and weekly canvassing to build opposition to the project; stories of mutual aid in the forest and jail vigils for arrested comrades; stories of everyday residents and neighbors coming together to fight for a different future in Atlanta. And those stories all matter.

But one of the stories that I find most hopeful in this moment is how the movement has responded to losses. Time and again, the Stop Cop City movement has taught me that what seems like a final loss can often be transformed into a beginning. You never know when you can turn a moment of would-be defeat into another opportunity to fight; a chance to live another day, to keep hope alive, to preserve the possibility of long term victory. And that alone makes the fight worth it.

Throughout the first summer of the movement, a coalition formed to canvass neighborhoods around the forest and to build public opposition to the plan. Through marches, petition circulation, call-in campaigns, and public comment, Atlanta residents voiced their opposition to the plan. In August 2021, the proposal came before the Atlanta City Council for a final vote. Many thought the plan would pass on that day. I certainly did. But at the last minute, and after significant public comment, the council member closest to the site objected to the plan on the grounds that the Atlanta Police Foundation had not reached out to her at all—compounding mounting accusations that APF's entire process was shrouded in secrecy. The plan was narrowly delayed by a vote of eight to seven—a result most had considered unlikely on the morning of the vote.

This was just one of many small wins that the movement was able to secure—moments where struggle in the face of unlikely odds nonetheless achieved a minor victory, making the state's repressive work harder and delaying defeat in a way that gave organizers more time to fight.

Despite the delay to the project, the city council nonetheless approved the plan by a ten-to-four vote in September 2021. They did so after listening to seventeen hours of public comment in which two-thirds of commenters stridently opposed the plan—a fact that would be referenced repeatedly in the following years as the project's anti-democratic nature became even clearer.

The approval vote was a major blow to the movement. That September day could have been the movement's end. Indeed, legislative defeats are often moments where coalitions fall apart, where despair sets in, where it seems we've lost and should move onto the next fight. And for many who had been organizing that summer, there was a necessary period of rest and recovery. No one can or should organize endlessly.

But while some regrouped, a new tactic emerged as forest defenders took to the Weelaunee Forest to physically defend it against destruction—a tactic that would endure successfully for nearly a year and a half and bring new life and creativity to the movement.

In other words, that September vote was the first major moment where what the state had hoped would be a death blow to the movement instead became an early setback within a protracted struggle—a time when the movement transformed a would-be end into a new beginning. A chance to fight again; to become more militant, more passionate, and more equipped to adequately respond to the stakes.

Just as importantly, despite the summer ending with a setback, organizers managed to lay many building blocks of what would become an international movement. Local opposition to the project grew. Militant acts of sabotage against companies backing the project quietly began. Activists generated hours of public comment and multiple media scandals. Movement journalists uncovered emails that began to illustrate the depths of collusion between APF, the city's corporations, and city leadership. And the movement peeled off four council votes from what would have otherwise likely been unanimous support for the project.

None of this was "enough" to defeat Cop City. But it all mattered, and its ripple effects would be felt for years to come.

The resistance continued in the following years as activists continued to occupy the forest, sabotage construction machinery, and shape the public narrative. As the forest defenders successfully delayed the timeline and heightened the cost of the project (originally projected to open in spring 2023, the project's construction was, by the end of 2022, almost two years behind schedule!), the powerful coalition of actors behind Cop City became more desperate. And, as is so often the case, the state's desperation translated to repression. Small armies of police officers gradually increased the frequency and aggression of raids in attempts to clear out forest defenders and make way for the forest's destruction.

But repression continued to breed more resistance, and more creativity. Activists called for weeks of action targeting corporations behind the project and companies contracted to build Cop City, with activists protesting outside the homes of CEOs while others destroyed construction machinery. Momentum continued to build.

On January 18, 2023, what many had feared came to pass: after roughly a month of escalating raids, a joint police task force marched into the forest and murdered forest defender Tortuguita in cold blood. Tortuguita, only twenty-six years old, was by all accounts full of love and determined to contribute to a future without police, prisons, or capitalism. On the same day, police arrested seven more people and charged them with domestic terrorism.

The January raid, too, could have been a moment when the movement ended. The forest was cleared out. The police had made clear that they were willing not only to conduct political assassinations of activists, but to follow those assassinations with smear campaigns attempting to blame the murdered for their own death.

But once again, the people said no. People took to the streets in Atlanta and in cities across the country in a night of rage. In Atlanta, a police cruiser was burned, surveillance cameras were smashed, and the windows of corporate backers of the project were broken. The police responded with more "domestic terrorism" arrests, but the message was clear: the people would not back down.

Once more, a moment that could have been the end instead became another installment in the struggle. Eventually, forest defenders retook the forest. Marches grew. National nonprofits that had lagged in their support and attention for the struggle finally began to take stands. The movement had firmly seized the public narrative, and city leadership realized just how insufficient their propaganda efforts had been thus far.

In response, police continued to escalate their repression, including a mass arrest of over forty people in March 2023 and charges against twenty-three of them for domestic terrorism—connected to a music festival in the forest, during which a nearby surveillance outpost associated with the construction efforts was burned roughly a mile away.

We witnessed these moments in horror, and sometimes despair. We watched as our comrades were kidnapped by police, taken to jail, and charged with outrageous crimes. We watched judges callously deny bond despite a total lack of credible evidence. We saw the city's propaganda machine begin to step up its game, trotting out well-worn "outside agitator" narratives in attempts to discredit protestors. We saw the deeply bipartisan consensus to criminalize the movement out of existence through state violence.

Even still, the movement continued to grow. In June 2023, Atlanta residents shattered previous records for in-person public comment, speaking for hours on end at City Hall against the proposed $67 million in public funding for Cop City. To no one's surprise, the Atlanta City Council ignored their residents, voting shortly after the close of public comment to approve the funding by eleven to four.

Unlike after the September 2021 vote, this time there was no question as to whether the movement would go on. In fact, there were already multiple plans in motion for new tactics following the June 2023 funding vote.

Just two days after the vote, a new coalition of organizations announced a new effort: a referendum to put Cop City to a direct vote by Atlanta residents. It was, admittedly, an imperfect tactic—who would trust the state to oversee a "democratic" process when the state had already made clear it would not heed the wishes of its residents? But it was another installment in the struggle, another opportunity to win—or at least to delay defeat. At the same time, others announced another week of action for the end of June 2023, making clear that militant direct action would continue over the summer (and it did!). The fight would continue on all fronts.

As of this writing, the movement is ongoing. And the situation often feels really bleak. The state always seems to have an answer for our maneuvers. Nothing that we've done so far has defeated Cop City. We have sustained massive losses and violence. Tortuguita was murdered. Sixty-one people face RICO charges. Many more have been arrested and brutalized by the police. Parts of the forest have been clear cut. Construction has begun, with claims that Cop City will open within months. City leadership continues to invest further in policing and surveillance.

But even as we grieve our losses, we should take stock of our wins—not in a way that lets us off the hook for the work of liberation or that provides hollow comfort, but for the ways in which we've won the chance to fight another day. The power that we've built. The consciousnesses we've raised. The people we've radicalized. The narratives we've shaped. The 116,000 signatures we gathered to force a vote on Cop City. The contractors we've forced to pull out of the project. The money-laundering charges we forced the attorney general to drop. The headaches we've caused for powerful people. The relationships we've built. The moments we bounced back. The solidarity we've cultivated. The scandals we've exposed. The power dynamics we've laid bare. The times where we've managed to lose a battle in a way that better sets us up to win the war. The tactics we've used to move ourselves a little closer to victory than we were before.

We can also look to past struggles that have ended in what we might call defeat, and understand how they nonetheless laid the groundwork for future fights. While the #NoCopAcademy campaign in Chicago did not manage to defeat the Cop Academy proposal, Stop Cop City organizers capitalized on lessons learned by No Cop Academy organizers as our movement began. Similarly, the Stop Cop City struggle has already fertilized the soil for struggles against proposed cop cities in other states—and organizers are now actively building campaigns in Charlotte, New York City, Baltimore, and elsewhere.

Perhaps no one better demonstrates the power of struggle in the face of loss than Belkis Terán, Tortuguita's mother. Since losing her child, Belkis has become the "mother of the movement," frequently sharing that while she lost Tortuguita, she gained hundreds of children who are fighting to stop Cop City. As Belkis told a crowd one day, even amid the losses and devastation, we are ultimately fighting for life: "Stop Cop City is a project for life. . . . We are all together in this project of life. We are not terrorists. We are not bad people. We want the best for the children in the future. . . . We have to think of the children of our grandchildren, because the earth is becoming an unlivable place. So we have to stop Cop City, because they are doing wrong, and the police are evil." As Belkis, someone who suffered the immeasurable loss of her child, puts so clearly: in the face of devastation, we can always recommit to the project of life.

None of this changes what I expressed in the opening words of this letter: things feel really horrible! But even as you take in the horror around you, I hope you will be able to remember—and to remind me, and to remind others—that we are all we have. That we are reason enough to keep fighting, even or especially when things are unimaginably awful. That fighting doesn't guarantee that we'll win, but that it gives us a chance of winning. That it's worth it to keep fighting even in the face of massive loss. And that even when we lose, we can turn moments of defeat into new opportunities to fight.

At whatever the end is—whether it's the end of my life, or the apocalyptic end of the world—I want to be able to say that I fought until the end. I hope you will too.

In love and solidarity,
Micah

Micah Herskind is an organizer, writer, and law student. He is a coeditor of *No Cop City, No Cop World: Lessons from the Movement* (Haymarket Books, 2025) and has organized in movements to Stop Cop City and close the Atlanta city jail.

Read This if Someone You Loved Has Killed Themself or Wants to, and Maybe You Want to Too but You Also Want to Survive

Leah Lakshmi Piepzna-Samarasinha

Trigger warning for discussion of suicide and childhood sexual abuse.

A note, written November 12, 2024:
I wrote this piece before Trump was elected for the second time, and what I wrote was true then. What is true now is that a storm that was coming is here, and a lot more people are going to kill themselves or struggle with wanting to over the next four years. Trans people, kids, disabled people, all our people. We are going to be forced to withstand a lot more utterly depraved brutality than we can stand. For some of us, it will flare our existing crazy, or make it more intense, intense in new ways. The overwhelm we are in may continue to push us to spin out and lash out at each other and ourselves.

I didn't ask for this particular batshit lab to examine how we really survive, none of us did, but this is what we got. My friend DuiJi quoted a line from Blu and Exile's song "So(ul) Amazin'" this morning: "My people need hope, and I'm the one with it." As much as the things I write about in this letter are hard, I think this letter also has hope in it—because I think being honest about the hard real things are a piece of what will help us make it through.

●

Dear X / disability justice organizer / DJ regular person / someone who doesn't call yourself "that word" / someone who is in community with disabled, Mad, and neurodivergent people and is trying to do the right thing and not sure of how:

So your friend / comrade / person you knew but not that well, Y, just killed themself. And you are devastated and in shock. Or numb as fuck. Or you don't know what you feel. Or it's one more stone of *this shit again* in your chest.

And maybe part of you is, like, maybe they did finally find peace for their pain. Maybe they are better off out of the hell of this world. And then you feel horrible for feeling that way. And you are so angry that the people and forces that led to their suicidality—their rapists, the fascists—keep walking around just fine. And you don't know what to do.

And maybe you're feeling really guilty. Feeling like you should've known, or, like, should've known what to do, the Rubik's cube combo that would have helped them find their way out of the trap. Kicking yourself, you should've picked up the phone. More. Wondering if you should've 5150'd them.[1] Wondering if you 5150'ing them would be what made them do it.

And maybe their death means your own suicidality is getting pinged. Or you're worried about if everyone else is going to want to kill themself now. Do you know that "suicide PTSD" is a thing? I didn't, til recently, but I sure have it. The PTSD you get from being the one who survives a lot of other people dying.

And maybe some people were really mad at them when they died, for shit they'd done at the end that didn't make sense or that pushed everyone's last nerve, was so cunty in its *I will do what I want, fuck you* or was actually hurting other people. Maybe you were angry at them because they were so determined to die and it scared the shit out of you, and it was easier being mad than saying how aching and scared you were. Probably you don't feel like you can say that you're angry.

You are so tired. This isn't your first time at the rodeo; it's your eight millionth. Or maybe it is your first one. Either way, you don't know what to do.

---

1. In California (and elsewhere) 5150 is slang for bringing someone to the psych ward without their consent. Every state has different slang for this based on the local law, somehow I've heard 5150 in many parts of the U.S. and Canada so it's what I use.

And you have to text everyone those "please call me, I can't tell you this news on text" texts, then sit with everyone who calls back, their anger or tears or what? or disbelief or numb. You have to help organize the memorial and figure out how to get into the storage unit. But right now, you have a thousand-mile stare, and you just want to crawl under your blankets into a thousand-mile hole in the ground.

And they're not there anymore to do the part of the work that they did, that only they could do.

And this was your homie. This was someone you'd known and worked with for years. This is someone who saved your life before. This is someone you love.

And/or: Maybe before they died, or period, Y got really fucking weird in the brain. Not "just" depressed but, like, doing things that you didn't know what to do with. Lashing out at other people. Spending money from the account. Saying shit that wasn't true that got more and more wild. Threatening people, maybe doxxing people. Sending a million messages. Just rampaging.

This is where the rubber hits the DJ-meets-TJ road.[2] This is shit we talk about privately that's very hard to talk about even privately, that we almost never talk about publicly. Because it's private. Because part of how crazy people keep each other safe is not ratting each other out in talking about our stigmatized, wild shit. Because we are still swimming against a massive tide of shit of unilateral demonization of crazy and crazy people; that we are all killers, *gasp*; or she has *that disorder*. You know.

We keep us safe. Strong communities make the police obsolete. We are more than the worst thing we've done. No one is disposable. Mad Pride.

All those phrases are real. And then, we have to figure out what they mean in practice.

---

2. TJ, short for transformative justice, a BIPOC feminist survivor-led movement creating strategies that create safety, justice, and healing for survivors of violence without primarily relying on the state, police, or prisons.

My friend said to me once, when I was coming to her for support with a really, really nuclear-hard situation where someone I had cared about had lost it and was lashing out at approximately five million people but especially me, including doxxing and stalking: *I can't promise to give you the solution, but I can try to give you the next right question.*

So in this essay, I'm not going to promise to fix it for you or give you a nice five-step solution. I'm going give you a status report. Tell you some stories I've seen and been in lately, some things I know. I'm going to talk about the next questions I've had, that I'm still in.

1. status report

Right now, it's a time on the clock of the world where a lot of people are having a really fucking hard time. It's not a binary, where some people have totally lost their shit and some of us are "okay." None of us are "okay," and there's a continuum we waver back and forth across, where we undulate from hanging in there, to struggling, to crisis, to back. There is no sane *us* and no insane *them*, though some of us are more seriously mentally interesting than others, and some of us are able to hide it more.

And, there are more people than I have seen in a minute who are some version of not okay where they, we, lash out at the people closest to them/us. Sometimes the people doing the lashing lash out at the people they love or are close to because they know we are abolitionists and won't call the cops.

It's really fun (sarcasm). And I'm still not going to call the cops (or the psych cops) on anybody, but sometimes the reality I am living through is deeply unpleasant. And then we have to organize in it. The *we* are who lashing out and in crisis, and the *we* who maybe are too, but not quite as hard at that moment.

What's the abolitionist way of handling it, that doesn't throw anyone away, yadda yadda, but where I am part of the *us* that we keep safe? What's the way of being accountable that doesn't throw the person causing harm who's ND under the bus pile, and still, we get to be accountable while still being nuts?

2

I'll tell you another story.

It was my friend's birthday the other day. My friend S, who killed himself last summer. I found out a couple days after he did it. One of our mutual friends texted me and told me to call her, she had news she couldn't text. I pulled over by the side of the highway in Connecticut where I was driving to the big disability justice arts festival happening on summer solstice, and she told me. He left us, honey.

I kept driving. I made it to the festival where my job was to build a big disabled grief altar installation in the courtyard, images of our dead and candles and flowers and little lights, so we could mourn all our beloved dead at this COVID-safer outdoor gathering, disabled kin together. It was the first time a lot of us had been with other people in person, in a non-Zoom gathering, in years. Me included. Some of us hadn't left our apartments for anything but doctor's appointments in years. Somehow, there they were, my friends who had kept me alive on Zoom for the past three.

I broke down when I had to put his photo on the damn altar. A friend on either side of me, my tears came down like milk in a tit, ugly and spitting, in a way they hadn't been able to with all the deaths I'd mourned in lockdown, alone. "How much more can we take?" My voice broke. Not dramatic. A real question.

2.5

The thing about being crazy and poor and working with others who are the same is, it's different than other forms of "organizing."

In what I didn't know would be the last year he would be alive, our friend was doing shit that drove me up a wall and made me rant to friends on text. He wasn't doxxing people, but he was posting all the time and using a lot of exclamation marks. He was saying "I did an oops," but some of the "oops" was that he was spending money that wasn't his while he was in an altered state. He was texting me wild shit. I was getting so many phone calls and texts, from him and about him, at every hour. His partnership was breaking up. He was in an extremely high level of physical pain at all times that doctors scratched their head at. He was burning down a lot of his closest relationships. He was buying diamond jewelry on the internet and then losing it in the emergency room. Was he breaking through to a next level of healing or was everything in his life going to hell? Unclear. What was clear was there was a lot of chaos.

He was my friend of twenty years, someone I'd known since LiveJournal. I knew him when he was sleeping in his car. I knew him when he was stuck in Hawaii in an abusive relationship. I knew him when we started—the collective "we"—making DJ space online and in person and finding each other, and he was part of that. I knew him when I was losing my shit and drove to his city, three hours away, to try and shake it off, where he met me at a now-RIP tea shop and bought me a cup and gave me a little zippered porch full of DBT flash cards, tea bags, and crystals he'd made and held my hand with compassion while I cried and shook.[3]

Then I was part of a group that was trying to start a space for a cohort of rising BIPOC disabled organizers in his home state and he was part of it. I watched him become an incredible organizer, someone who figured out how to get the city to give poor disabled people thousands of dollars in gift cards during early COVID, someone who hung in there through the kinds of two hundred-comment threads of people screaming at each other that

---

3. DBT: Dialectical Behavioral Therapy.

turn my hair white. He knew how to bring people together, how to talk to everyone without condescending or being weird to people who were new to activism. He organized a massive, successful DJ conference that people attended from all over the world, even when it had to get postponed twice because he and half the conference had to flee wildfire smoke by driving to another state. When he finally got stable housing at his lover's after years of homelessness, they opened their home to people who needed housing, people sleeping in their van in the driveway and in the spare room.

And then he was in a pain crisis. And then he was in a mental health crisis. And he didn't always feel like he could be honest to the funder, to the other organizers, to the people he was supporting, about just how bad it was. Containment practice. Not wanting to blow things up. Privacy. *I'm ok*. And then he was crashing and burning so hard.

And, we are more than our worst thing, but he was doing some worst things. He was a whole person, but he wasn't okay, and I didn't know what to do, and I did not have enough time to figure it out because I had a lot of shit going on, what with my own dead and dying parents and partnership bust-up and cross-country moves and all. What with my own sick and crazy, and with my own being newly in recovery in Al Anon and trying to stop myself from being the automatic fix-it femme, from having a mammalian diving reflex always running toward the burning building. I loved him. I was trying to have healthy boundaries. I was trying to put on my own oxygen mask first, all that shit we say to each other. I was angry at him sometimes. I was scared for him. I was listening to people who had been close to him but who were really angry and hurt at things he had done. I was exhausted. I didn't know what to do.

I ranted to my friend about the whole situation, a friend I first met when they were a queer youth in the queer and trans youth writing club I taught at the community centre, now a grown artist peer, someone who has led me through the valley of the shadow of death aka taken my twenty-minute-long long ass podcast-length voice memos when I was losing it. They reminded me that any time you're working with other people who've never had any money, who have been sleeping in their car or living on $1,080 a month, or $795, or $395, and they get sent a $5,000 project grant, there is a not-small chance that one of their inner little parts might want to buy some shiny shit with it when they have the credit card number. Who wouldn't? Another friend was like, "Do you know how many times we've had to explain to the funders that, yeah, the gift cards got blown on something else?"

This is what it is to work with other poor and crazy people. Shit happens. Middle-class, normal people have their parents to buy them shiny shit. We have nothing, and then we have "Maybe organizing will save our lives and get us some food security," and the most money we have ever seen in our lives, and so much pressure to get it right. Shit happens. We blow the money, but we also sometimes blow up our lives when we are finally "succeeding."

2.75

S had dissociative parts. So do I. We both survived the kind of incest that even some incest people put their hand over their mouth when they hear about it. I have memories that I'm not supposed to be able to have, of my genitals being touched and penetrated before I could talk. My friend's parents locked him in a closet and pimped him out from when he was small. Pieces of ourselves broke off to hold the unholdable experiences, and the things that were forbidden to us, like rage.

We survive that way. And we live having survived the worst things in the world via a brilliant bodymind hack that is so deeply stigmatized. If we're really lucky, we find other people who are on the disassociation continuum too, who can help us find our way through the valley of the shadow of shit to somehow not hating ourselves. But that takes a lot of luck.

I spent a lot of July 2021 on the phone with S. One of the

times he went to Sunshine, the mega-psych ward in his city. He was in the highest-lockdown ward, but he still managed to try to kill himself with the bedsheets. "That's what they're for!" he chirped. S was a real OG of crazy. I was on my porch couch a lot that month talking to him on the ward phone. A lot of our texts and calls were about being plural. I was trying to tell him the exiles and protectors deserved a medal. He said, "Yeah, yeah," but he wasn't convinced.

If there's one thing I know, it's parts shame. If there's one thing I know, it's how fucking hard it is to get even not-completely-fucked care when you have parts/are plural/are multiple/have DID. If there's one thing I remember, it's that there's messages from him in 2022 saying his therapist was firing him, saying he needed a higher level of care than outpatient could provide. That was no doubt fucking true, but it didn't exist. Sunshine stopped admitting him, saying they couldn't help him. So, then what? Who could?

In May 2022, when I'd first moved back to Massachusetts, he asked what I thought about him getting an Airbnb and trying to do McLean's partial hospitalization program. I gave him what info I had: *I've heard it's bad. If they do DID stuff, I get why you're thinking about it—MA can be a lot of things. Will MassHealth accept an Airbnb as residency or give you shit?* Looking back, it's clear he was maybe trying to say: *I am fucking desperate. I've been at level 11 physical pain for over a year. I have a Dilaudid patch and it's still not working kind-of-thing. I'm literally going crazy, and there's no place in my state that says they can help me.* You have to be pretty desperate to consider flying across the country to get to an Airbnb to go to the hospital that was featured in *Girl, Interrupted*.

In case it's not obvious, I am angry at his therapists who fired him, Sunshine for refusing to admit him, and, most of all, his parents for sexually abusing him as a small child. In case it's not obvious, I'm really glad I knew S. I still have those DBT cards he gave me in a cute little pink print cloth zippered pouch in my dresser's smallest drawer. The "protection from suicidal ideation" card he gave me rides shotgun in my wallet every day.

2.85

And I also think: How fucked is it if he thought he had one shot to get out of poverty and the thing that was saving him also killed him? He had been so cash poor for his whole life, and he was a really good organizer for a long time, and he was like, *this is the one thing that could get me to long-term survival—organizing.*

I don't think the stress of doing it, or community dynamics, are solely why he killed himself. And I think he is responsible for the harm he caused.

But there's this trope I see of "You do it so well, you're so there for folks, you're infallible," that's seductive. And I think to a degree some of his helper parts were running the show past what he could do—as we do—and then he would just crash.

I don't know—when you're super crazy and you become a disabled or Mad organizer and you are good at it, and then everyone is screaming at you out of bottomless need that's never been filled, and you are also having a really hard fucking time, there is immense pressure to never fuck up. To be a "good crazy," if you're going to be crazy, the kind who is never actually crazy. S was definitely really crazy, and I think he felt such shame when it showed. S was definitely really crazy and worked so hard to mask it, to have his more together parts be up front. And I know from perma-masking that there's always a crash after. Sometimes just a regular crash, sometimes a crash where you flame out into the flip side of the perfect one.

And when your one ticket out of poverty and desperation is being a crazy organizer, but there is pressure on you to never be crazy and you shame-spiral the fuck out when you do—what then?

That pressure to be perfect and that one-shot-out, it probably doesn't give as much chances for accessible accountability as one would like.

3. a sidenote

I don't want to write about the other part I mentioned in the opener of this piece. The part about people who are or were our kin who got lost, who are lashing out, who are in a rage and acting abusively, and whose behavior partially dovetails with being in an altered state. Where I'm like, *I don't know if you're COINTELPRO, but you don't have to be causing the kind of damage you are.*

I don't know how to write about it; because there's the TJ and de-escalation I know how to do; and then there's people who do some so-completely wild shit who are partially in another reality, and I didn't know what to do about that besides, after sincerely offering them resources and other choices and getting screamed at, de-escalate, disengage, do digital and personal security, do not get sucked in, let people know what's going on so we can build a web of safety, and personal spiritual protection.

I did all those things, and they did keep me safer. I spent hundreds of hours sweating it alone and with others, trying to figure out what the disability justice response was to someone who relentlessly stalked, terrorized, harassed, and finally doxxed me for two and a half years. I finally realized that part of the DJ thing to do was to act as if me, a disabled brown femme, was worth protecting.

I finally got a protection order against them—where we were based, you can do it without involving the police. The community intervention we tried didn't fail. Because all of them increased the safety I felt, but they also didn't make the stalking stop. Two and a half years of panic attacks and this person flooding every gig and every person I'd worked with for the past twenty years with thousands of DMs and emails, I still did not want to use any part of the system. I went to it as a broken last resort when the stalker started talking about my parents and what grade school I'd gone to and posting my legal last name on the internet.

I survived stalking and DV as a twenty-something and it makes me so tired to be almost fifty and be facing the same thing.

I didn't promise you an answer, but I want to have more answers than I have. Maybe for now, it will be helpful enough to read that if you've experienced this—someone in community going buck and turning on you, and not a goddamn thing you or other people do to offer resource and set boundaries makes them stop—you are not alone. To hear that no matter how ND someone is, we always still have choices about how we act. That in a busted world, we use all the imperfect tools we have at our disposal to live. That figuring out anti-ablest forms of accountability is going to be a long bop. And sometimes the best fix we have isn't sitting and explaining and offering and being endlessly patient. Sometimes the DJ approach to someone wilding out is finally just saying: No.

4

Next year, it will be a decade since beloved Black femme artist and educator Taueret Davis killed herself. Her suicide ushered in what I call in my head "the femme suicide years," a super-intense two years and change where another iconic femme killed her, him, or themself every six months. The femme suicide years opened up a decade of more communities talking about suicide, Madness, altered states, suicidality, and crisis. Mad people continued to organize around these issues, as we have always done, and well-meaning abolitionist allies at times tried to do that work too—sometimes without us or our input. A decade later there are more skills, more Mad-led projects, more crisis lines that don't call the cops, less of a sense that Madness, suicide, and crisis are dirty jokes or hot gossip. And yet.

I can't believe it's been a decade, her memorial card is still on my ancestor altar, which is thick and now covers the whole top of one of my dressers. It feels like a minute ago that she died, Obama was still president and we were all crowded into a Brooklyn collective queer house, eating donated banana pudding, learning to organize our first memorial for her, me slinging weed brownies my lover had made out of my bra to help grieving femmes at her funeral get through it.

I am someone who has been suicidal off and on all my life, more intensely when I was younger. In my forties, honestly, Taueret's death was part of it, that lessened. When she died, it was like a baby turned around in the womb, and all of a sudden I was like: *no matter what, no matter how bad I want it sometimes, I can't kill myself. I'll let myself get locked up if I don't have any other way to stay here. Even if I don't want to live for myself right then, I can't fuck up everyone else I'll leave behind.* I've been studying suicide and sitting with suicide and emailing out the how not to die when you really want to die tips to people who really want to die, before and since. There's people who I thought we were gonna lose who we didn't. There's people I never thought were going to go who did. There's people we didn't know how to save. (The idea of saving is false.)

For the last five pandemic years, deaths have stripped so many leaves from my tree, suicidal and not and some places in between, and the way I and others I watch feel about death has shifted. Sometimes I understand differently now, why people want to get the fuck out. It's hard to talk about when we are fighting against the legalization of medical assistance in dying (MAiD) and state-legislated death, insisting on our right to stay here.

But sometimes, while fighting for our ability to stay here and a world that we want to fucking stay in, I still can see the portal in the sky so clear, clearer than it was before everybody died and everything got so fucking hard, see how tempting it might be to go up it. It's so fucked up down here, and the clouds are a house-party couch full of people I loved the best. My ancestor altar thick with ghost friends, my calendar studded with birthdays, death days, days we found out, little shocks and grief anniversary days all the time, days I have to log out of work early and go cry in my car, days I don't know why I'm sad, days where I do the checking in with the whole fam. I stay here. I understand why people might assess their chances and choices and go, *bye*.

Reading this piece, my friend Elliot Fukui said, "I spent a

decade being like, *stay here*, but also I'm recognizing people's agency to make a choice in this moment. . . I had a little breakdown the other day where I was like, I spent years keeping people alive for what? Being kept alive to be deported, to be hungry, to lose your health care, to be exploited by your employer? What does it mean to want to survive under these conditions?"[4]

●

I promised you I wouldn't lie to you. I promised you I wouldn't give you a fake little platitude. I promised you I would give you the next question(s). I promised you I would give you the truth. I promised I would tell you a story. The story I am telling you is messy and doesn't have a nice ending where it always comes out different through community care.

What I am saying is that when you are a crazy, broke, survivor disabled person, sometimes This Is Disability Justice. You're gonna fight like hell for us all to stay alive, and people are going to die anyway, in completely random, predictably unpredictable ways. Not your fault. Your gravestone to tend.

I worry so much about, as DJ continues and progresses, that there's such pressure on people to be disabled organizers without somehow being disabled or nuts or neurodivergent anymore. Especially when people are poor and there is sometimes Organizer/Be on a Panel/Consultant/Grant money around, there is so much pressure to somehow be Competent—when we got into this thing because we, you know, weren't.

So don't do that. Don't make movements where people have to be perfect and never lose it to be leaders. Including you. Make space for us all to be that crazy sometimes. Make ways to love people who are crazy and still be like, "friend—not okay," when something we do is not okay.

---

4. Voice memo, Elliot Fukui, April 7, 2025.

Back in '08, I was in a three-day training held by Generation 5, an OG transformative justice organization whose goal was to end childhood sexual abuse in five generations without using the state. It blew my mind. It was one of the first trainings where I heard someone talk about how CSA holds up every oppressive system that exists, from Christian supremacy to ableism. It was also the first place I ever heard someone talk about somatics, and the trainer, explaining what somatics was and why we should care, had said, "As things get worse in the world, we're going to be forced to experience more and more intense sensations."[5]

It's sixteen years later, and we indeed are being forced to withstand more extreme intensity all the time. I did a lot of cut-rate somatic therapy that was DIY brain surgery, that rebuilt my bodymind from the inside out. I don't float out my body so much anymore like I used to. But even with all that, the degree of wall of fire genocidal bullshit we are forced to endure and witness is beyond many of my apocalyptic dreams of years ago. Of course we'd want to leave our bodies, whether through disassociation, or through the knife's edge of wanting to go from this life.

But I still want us to survive, to make it to the other side. I want us to go through this fucking super-intense portal time and see what's waiting for us on the other side.

I hope you keep finding ways of withstanding. I hope you find ways to stay. I have told some of these true stories hoping they are a bitter fire to warm your hands by. I hope you can find, again, the suicide skills and strategies you already know, that we

---

5. Broadly defined, somatics are body-based therapeutic approaches to addressing ways trauma freezes you into triggers or shame or automatic reactions, and help people increase capacity to stay present in hard situations/sensations. Somatics, Generative Somatics in particular, became widely popular in certain 2010s left movements that were attempting to address how oh yeah, we're all traumatized and it fucks us and our movements up unless we deal with it.

already made. The secret DJ TJ languages made from the rubber that already hit the road. The soft hard skills, grist from all that millstone grinding.

Build on them. Tell others about them. Pass the suicide survival tips back and forth. Tell your own honest as fuck stories about the real crazy hard. Keep telling them. Find your ways to stay here, imperfectly, honestly.

Perhaps, if we all do, we will keep finding ways to stay.

With love and in community,
Leah

Leah Lakshmi Piepzna-Samarasinha (they/she) is an older cousin, regular person, memory worker, disability and transformative justice uncle bytch, and the author or coeditor of ten books including *The Future Is Disabled* (coedited with Ejeris Dixon; Arsenal Pulp Press, 2022), *Beyond Survival: Strategies and Stories from the Transformative Justice Movement* (AK Press, 2020), *Care Work: Dreaming Disability Justice* (Arsenal Pulp Press, 2018), *Tonguebreaker* (Arsenal Pulp Press, 2019), and *Dirty River* (Arsenal, 2016). A 2020–2021 Disability Futures Fellow, Lambda and Jeanne Córdova Award winner, five-time Publishing Triangle short-lister, and longtime disabled QTBIPOC space maker, they are currently building Living Altars, a cultural space by and for disabled QTBIPOC writers.

Tools

Fireweed Collective: Crisis Toolkit and Online Groups
https://fireweedcollective.org/crisis-toolkit
https://fireweedcollective.org/support-groups
Suicide Intervention (For Weirdos, Freaks, and Queers), zine and workshop by Carly Boyce
https://www.tinylantern.net/suicide-intervention-resources

Wildflower Alliance Peer Support
https://wildfloweralliance.org
Mad Queer Organizing Strategies
https://madqueer.org

Writings

Thom, Kai Cheng, "stop letting trans girls kill ourselves / not a poem," *sintrayda* (blog), November 2, 2016, sintrayda.tumblr.com.
Stanford, Rashni "Scrambling Time and Collapsing Space,"*Syanpses, Deep Space Mind 215* (blog), May 11, 2024, deepspacemind215.substack.com.
    Wright, Cortez, "Learning to Live with Wanting to Die," *The Body Is Not an Apology* (blog), June 10, 2015, thebodyisnotanapology.tumblr.com.
    Stephens, Morgan, "Down In The Well, We Will Mourn and Sing: Surviving Mental Illness," in *The Long COVID Survival Guide*, ed. Fiona Lowenstein (New York: The Experiment, 2022).
    "Suicidal Ideation 2.0" and "Femme Suicide Strategies," in Leah Lakshmi Piepzna-Samarasinha, *Care Work* (Arsenal Pulp Press, 2018).

Crisis Lines That Don't Call the Cops

Call Blackline
https://www.callblackline.com
Trans Lifeline
https://translifeline.org
THRIVE Lifeline
https://thrivelifeline.org
Relationships Evolving Possibilities
https://repformn.org
MH First Oakland, a project of Anti-Police-Terror Project
https://www.antipoliceterrorproject.org/mh-first-oakland

The Network/ LA Red
https://www.tnlr.org/en/
Directory of Peer Respites in the US:
https://power2u.org/directory-of-peer-respites/
Peer respites are non-carceral, non-forced treatment spaces where people experiencing emotional crisis or altered mental states can go and receive food, support, care, meds hookups if wanted, other forms of alternative healing, and often peer support from other Mad people who have experienced similar.

Read This if You Are Struggling with Your Mental Health

Aaron Goggans

Dear Beloved,

(For that is what you are, even though we have never met. You are loved.)

This letter is for anyone struggling with their mental health in the movement. Maybe worrying if struggling with mental health in the movement makes them crazy.

In my experience as a neurodivergent organizer with a history of anxiety, mood swings, and nonnormative information processing, the line between mental illness and what Martin Luther King Jr. called being "creatively maladjusted" to society has never seemed clear to me. For King, we must never be well adjusted to injustice. It was a call to push back against the pathologizing of people who resisted their oppression. Our mental health, like our personalities and worldviews, are a result of some mix of nature, nurture, and social environment.

I think the same neurodivergence that can make us anxious in social situations, or hyper-fixate on details, or swing from grandiose thoughts to deep over-focus on flaws can often be part of what makes us good organizers. It's also the flip side of sensitivity that allows us to read situations well, plan ahead, or connect deeply with the world. I'm not suggesting that "mental illness is a super power" but that the same way of sensing, perceiving, and experiencing the world that makes our day-to-day lives challenging also helps us imagine and live into other worlds.

Those of us with diagnosable mental illness or neurodivergence (even if we don't have the means to be formally diagnosed) have had to live in the margins long enough to learn a thing or two about surviving while being creatively maladjusted. So, as someone who identifies as crazy, I'm going to be speaking to all of us who have become creatively maladjusted because I think the advice is equally relevant for those of us for whom mental illness is more temporary and situational and those of us for whom it is a lifelong reality.

With the rise of fascism, we are going to experience those in power using everything within their power to warp consensus reality. From news media to nonsensical laws or theatrical shows of force, they will try to twist everyone's worldview into one in which their actions are justified. This is frightening and literally produces anxiety and depression. In the coming years, lessons in how to thrive, learned by those of us who are born with a strong tendency to step outside consensus reality, might be lifesaving to more neurotypical organizers

Being an organizer means you have enough wisdom and experience to know that your community or nation (or the world) has some serious problems that no existing formation can fix but you think you might be able to convince enough other people to make the change. It also means that you push past the consensus reality, the eternal messaging that says, "Everything is fine," or "Okay, things are messed up, but you gotta leave these sorts of things to men in power."

Can you imagine a better definition of being creatively maladjusted than living outside the consensus reality? Add to that having the audacity not only to envision another world but to act, day in and day out, as if that world is as real as the world other people live in. To organize well is to live on an alternative timeline in which we get free, and to start acting as if you already are.

So again, if you find yourself wondering, after weeks or perhaps months of constant stress, maybe some panic attacks or lashing out at your comrades, or perhaps even waking up in the middle of the night terrified of jackboots at your door, if you are going crazy, I'd offer that maybe that's the wrong question. The better question is, how can we take care of our mental health while either refusing—or being just plain unable—to adjust ourselves to injustice?

So, now that we have set aside fears of being crazy, at least for a second, where do we go from here?

First: Tend to your body. Sleep, eat something hearty, get a hug, and touch earth. It may seem trite, especially if your mental health challenges arise—at least in part—from the stress of your movement work. These four things are a great place to start. We are basically big children. Or maybe more accurately, children are just small people who don't have coping mechanisms yet. Yet the reason that most kids' problems can be solved with a nap, food, a hug, or playing outside is not because their lives are simple but because those are the basic things all humans need to regulate our emotions.

Not to be too on the nose, but to be creatively maladjusted is a mercurial gift. Many of us have seen stress and trauma turn the shared reality of a tight-knit group of people into something toxic. I have distinct memories of supporting Black-led organizing collectives during the Breonna Taylor and George Floyd uprisings that have burned this realization into my soul.

I spent about three months in Louisville, Kentucky, during the height of the 2020 uprisings. By the time I arrived, the local activist community was already a hundred days into consecutive actions. That meant at least one action—though often more—every day for a hundred days. Many of these actions were banner drops or marches, but some included shutting down bridges or camping out on the front lawn of an elected official.

Activists and organizers were beaten, tear-gassed, and snatched off the street. They were woken up and questioned in the middle of the night. Still, they got up every morning, planned more actions, and ran a mutual aid network that fed hundreds (sometimes thousands) of residents a day. One hundred days turned a group of college students and young adults into committed revolutionaries—committed revolutionaries who were so paranoid that they wouldn't give their local activist group their social security number so that they could become an employee, because they didn't want the feds (who already knew who they were) to have that information.

They organized without pay for eighty hours a week. They ran a food-delivery service because the only grocery store on the Black side of the city had been closed after a Black man was killed on the property by the National Guard. They ran a housing program because developers were hiring police to evict Black residents from certain neighborhoods. They knew that without food, without housing, members of their community would die.

It took hours of conversations, constant reminders that they need to eat vegetables, and sometimes my refusal to meet with them until they slept for them to hear that if they did not stop, they might die. As my collective supported them in slowing down, we heard more and more about what the uprising had taken from them. How their affiliation with the protests had lost them jobs, or how something they tweeted got reposted by one of Trump's children, leading to someone finding out where they lived and kicking the door down.

They had formed what you might call trauma bonds with their idea of what movement was. A trauma bond is where someone feels deeply connected to their abuser because after the harm, the abuser lavishes love and praise on them to "make it okay" and promises never to do it again. The negative feelings of the abuse become closely connected to positive feelings that come from the lavishing of care, attention, and support that comes after. Eventually, our bodies can't distinguish well between the two, even if our minds can. Praise reminds us of the abuse and the abuse gets interpreted as love.

In the same way, cultures of self-sacrifice and disposability can creep into our movements. Many of us develop the misbelief that you must put your body and spirit on the line, often with no plan for how to care for yourself after. Then there is a picture of you at the protest that goes viral and people comment on how brave we are or talk about how this is a new civil rights movement and we are following in the footsteps of giants. At the debrief, the action organizers might even provide food, and that might be the only way you can afford to eat now that you've lost your job.

In many (though by no means all) movement spaces, destructive ideas about the nature of healing and restoration remain pervasive: that healing is the responsibility of individual organizers; that burnout is neither avoidable nor the organization or community's responsibility; that mental illness is a sign of inherent weakness. These false beliefs can keep you pushing through unnecessary pain, blaming yourself for your inability to get over it.

At the same time, there is no feeling better than a movement high. Even as I was supporting younger activists in Louisville, trying to encourage them to slow down, I was exhilarated by their energy. I felt compelled to push myself harder to support them, meeting them at any time of the day they needed me. I felt so seen and valuable when they would open up about how helpful our collective was. Even as I was tired, even as I was devastated by sitting with the family of a man killed by police as they read the letter from city hall blaming their child for their own death, I felt more alive than I have ever felt.

This cycle can create a weird world, a new reality, that only your equally creatively maladjusted activist friends understand. You can form such intense—if dysfunctional—bonds with your comrades that you seek to be with them all the time. Yet, in some cases, the only thing you do together is more traumatic actions. Eventually, activists find themselves passing harm back and forth, asking more and more of each other because they live in a world where the stakes are impossibly high. *The next action has to be bigger to justify all that we have sacrificed. You can't put your own needs for sleep or rest ahead of the movement, because if the movement is not worth our lives, then why did we give up everything for it?*

Unfortunately, there is also no low like a movement low. The depths of my usual depressive episodes cannot compare to the existential languishing that a movement conflict or setback can trigger in me. It's one thing to think your life is hopeless, but a badly executed action or a mass arrest can make it seem like the world will never improve. No matter how much your body hurts, no matter how hard it is to get out of bed, a movement depression will gaslight you into jumping back into the fire before you are ready.

A sleep-deprived, hungry brain can't see that the more you resource yourself, the more you will have to give; that an hour of work that comes after eight hours of sleep, a healthy interpersonal interaction, and equally healthy meal is going to be a hundred times more productive than an hour of work that comes after three weeks of little sleep and a Hot Cheetos–based diet.

An overwhelmed person who has been doing actions to avoid having the time to sit with their emotions is not going to see how much pain they cause when they lash out and chastise those who are not willing to sacrifice as much as them. They are unable to see that if they really paused and took stock of the cost, they wouldn't want to sacrifice any more either.

Like so many of us, I had to learn the hard way that every challenge we face is harder to deal with when we are tired, hungry, lonely, or have been stuck inside for long periods of time. It was only through losing myself to the movement, getting sick and never being quite the same again, that I realized self-care is crucial. I've come to think of these things as mental health hygiene—things you have to do every day to maintain as much of your health as you can. They won't fix anything on their own, but they at least they will slow the pace of things getting worse. These actions all increase our nervous system's ability to regulate itself.

"Dysregulation" is probably the best term I know to describe the deterioration of mental health. When you are dysregulated, your body can have unskillful or self-defeating reactions to stimuli. This could mean being irritable over small things or reading all social interaction for potential threats (i.e., experiencing paranoia). Yet it can also mean the opposite: a lack of response. It can mean not caring about the risks of a situation, feeling little empathy for others' pain, or having little interest in the things you used to love.

If you're an organizer, you have probably spent years being somewhat dysregulated. Unfortunately, many movement spaces have normalized dysregulation. So many overwork because if they stop, they can't help but notice all the uncomfortable feelings they have been bottling up inside. Our people might be open to risky actions because they can't really feel anything else and the chaos of risky actions are the only times they feel alive. Our people might only be able to see what is wrong with the situation, or why some choice is problematic. We can often write this off as "the curse of knowledge," but it can often be a narrowing of vision and rigidity that comes from unprocessed emotion.

For many of us, our dysregulation is complicated by trauma. "Trauma" is a word that gets tossed around a lot. It has gotten to the point where it seems like every social behavior is based in trauma. Personally, I believe that this is because, while not everything is trauma, trauma is everywhere. We live in a deeply traumatic society and at a particularly traumatic point in the history the planet's climate. I think of trauma as a time-traveling somatic (or embodied) experience. It is experienced when our bodies react to stimuli based on a story of previous harm in order to avoid or prevent future harm.

Trauma occurs when your fight, flight, freeze, or fawn response is triggered yet, for some reason, your body cannot release all the energy of that activation. Often this is an experience for which you have no context, something that is so extreme, foreign, or novel that you can't situate it in your story of self or story of the world. This is also why childhood trauma is so impactful: it occurs at the time where you have the least amount of personal context.

The danger might pass, but your body files away a somatic connection to whatever triggered the response so that the next time you experience the trigger, you respond in the way your body has learned to respond. In this sense, trauma is deeply tied to an overwhelming of one's capacity for self-regulation. Trauma can occur when you experience more activation than your system can effectively dissipate, or when the kind of activation you experience is something your body doesn't know how to handle.

As Resmaa Menakem writes in his book *My Grandmother's Hands*, "Contrary to what many people believe, trauma is not primarily an emotional response. Trauma always happens in the body. It is a spontaneous protective mechanism used by the body to stop or thwart further (or future) potential damage." A trauma response can be triggered by anything the body perceives as threat, rightly or wrongly. It is important to note that the brain experiences threat to social status the same way it deals with threats to the body. Somatically, the experiences are almost identical. This is why we say things like "I almost died of shame." Ego death—the destruction of things to which we cling in order to build a sense of self—is experienced somatically as a threat to life.

This means that if you have been dysregulated for months, you can be traumatized by things that wouldn't have affected you much if you were healthy. To me, this is a big reason movement conflicts are so volatile and frequent. It's a bunch of tired people whose long-standing unmet needs for sleep, food, connection, and validation are exacerbated by interactions with the police and with the strategies of reactions that are designed to increase stress. When conflict happens, it is primed to set off other pains, other time-traveling emotions, that are not connected to the conflict in question and thus cannot be fully resolved by resolving the disagreement that started the conflict in the first place.

Back in 2016, I was an organizer with Black Lives Matter DMV. The police put these bright flashing lights outside my and my sister's bedrooms. It was so bright that it was hard to sleep. It was a reactionary strategy developed by the Israeli military for use in Palestine. It brings to "community policing" a familiar interrogation (or what might more reasonably be called torture) technique: preventing detained people from sleeping. This lack of sleep wreaked havoc on my and my sister's relationships as we were just constantly cranky. It was not until we were able to make the connection to the lights that we could stop engaging in petty arguments and redirect our ire toward the cops. But that was easier said than done, given how much trauma we were accumulating together.

Now, it is crucial to state here that not all trauma is the same. Like most things, it exists on a spectrum. In the same way that some people will respond to a precipitating event with brief, mild depression and others might experience chronic episodes of crippling depression with no discernible trigger, trauma can be simple and worked through with deep breathing and thought stopping, or it can be complex and take years of therapy to recognize and even more years to lessen levels of activation (that may never completely go away).

Likewise, what traumatizes one person may barely affect another. While there are some events, like witnessing serious violence, that tend to be traumatic for most people, nearly anything that activates a sense of flight or fright can be traumatic.

If any of what I've said resonates with a conflict you are dealing with right now, then please eat a good meal, rest, get a hug from a safe person, and go outside. As organizers, it's so easy to fall into the cult of "maximal effort." We can rush into restorative or transformative processes, principled struggle, or even a defense posture because we think it's the ethical thing to do. Especially when we have caused harm, we can be worried that taking time to rest is selfish or avoiding accountability.

But hear me when I say: no one is served by your entering into or facilitating a process when you don't have the capacity to self-regulate. To do so is to run the risk of making things worse with unskillful action, or of opening up more pain than you have the capacity to process, leading to even more trauma. I can't tell you how many times I've seen so-called restorative spaces cause more harm than they were attempting to heal.

I once felt so responsible for a space I had helped organize that I tried to facilitate through a conflict on little sleep and with a facilitation team that was so triggered that they had checked out. In hindsight, everyone would have been better served by me just walking away. Instead, my maximal effort fed the conflict and led to me being asked to leave a space I had helped organize. It caused a rift in an organizing community that, half a decade later, hasn't fully healed.

That leads me to my last point. Whether a conflict is keeping you up at night, memories of an arrest cause you to lose time, or you experience anxiety at the thought of going to a meeting, you are not alone. I can assure you that another organizer has experienced something similar. Likewise, another organizer has been where you are and got the help they needed to make it through to the other side. There is no need to reinvent the wheel, and you don't get any bonus points for struggling alone.

Reach out, ask for help, and accept the help that is offered—especially when you think you are unworthy. Giving comrades opportunities to show up for us is an exercise in solidarity. Take all the naps. Eat all the food that makes you feel good. Find the people who make you feel safe and connected and ask them to help you regulate. Touch the earth.

It seems so small, but it's so crucial. About two weeks into supporting activists in Louisville, we realized that all our years of training in crisis intervention were sometimes less immediately helpful than just inviting people to drink some tea, cleaning their homes for them, and giving them a hug. We realized that telling people to rest is not enough. We had to make rest easy. We held meetings outside, letting people soak in the sun, feeding them solid meals, and then scheduling a two-hour break in rooms full of fluffy couches.

We realized, too, that many people didn't actually know how to self-regulate and weren't around anyone stable enough to coregulate with. So we incorporated groundings into every meeting. We started off with active grounding in music or pose making to help people release some of the energy that had been accumulating, before it could become trauma. As people's nervous systems calmed, we would introduce breathing exercises and guided meditation into the mix. To offer another way for people to regulate themselves, one elder began running Qigong lessons in the morning and evening.

We worked with leadership to ensure that there were no other meetings happening during grounding times. That way, all those traumatized activists who were afraid to be alone could gather around an activity that actually resourced them, rather than asking them to sacrifice more. Eventually, we were able to have more one-on-one relationships where we could ask each organizer what they used to do for fun, or what activities had brought them joy. We encouraged them to bring activities like coloring or singing by incorporating them into meeting agendas.

Once they connected with joy and saw how much more energy it brought them, we introduced something even more radical. What if we allowed ourselves joy just because joy connects us to what it means to be human? What if your joy or rest didn't have to make us more productive? For many, this idea was too radical. The idea of doing anything other than pushing harder was literally unthinkable.

Unfortunately, not all of us survived the uprising with our lives or with our spirits intact. Too many of our ancestors and peers gave everything to movements that refused to facilitate their rest or reconnection to joy. To borrow from Allen Ginsberg, we have seen some of the best minds of our generation destroyed by an under-resourced madness—a creative maladjustment that was not allowed to be human and to be resourced by joy, love, and connection and so turned in on itself.

The reality is that joy, laughter, and rest are not only the best medicine; they are also the best measurements of our mental health. To paraphrase Emma Goldman, if we are not laughing, dancing, or singing, there might be something wrong with our revolution. If there is one piece of advice I can give you in these perilous times, it's that sometimes your very maladaptiveness will be what keeps you from despair or, worse, accommodating fascism.

I think King was right to say that the fate of the world is in the hands of the creatively maladjusted. We cannot afford to adjust ourselves to the cruelty of fascism, the disposability of late-stage capitalism, or apathy of indifference to the plight of fellow humans. With the future in our hands, we must nurture our ability to see and live into new worlds by caring for each other and normalizing rest and joy.

In and love and solidarity,
Aaron

Aaron Goggans is an organizer, writer, and movement infrastructure builder, born and raised in Colorado. His politics were shaped by interfaith organizing in the Great Plains, labor and housing organizing on the South Side of Chicago, Black Liberation organizing in Washington, DC, and international delegations to Korea, Hong Kong, and South Africa. He is currently the Steward of the Pattern at the WildSeed Society, a Black-led, BIPOC-focused organization that supports movement stewards building a better world.

Read This if You Are Organizing Outside the Law
Brit "Red" Schulte

Dear Comrade,

    I've been an organizer for half of my life now. What a strange thing to write . . .

    I've been involved with struggles to abolish the death penalty, worked to kick racists and war criminals off campuses, to fund and expand abortion access, to form unions and strike committees. I've slept on concrete during youth rebellions, supported criminalized survivors of gender-based violence, taught people how to reverse overdoses and test their drugs, built peer education among sex workers toward decriminalizing our labor, organized too many vigils for fallen comrades, gotten arrested symbolically *and against all my best efforts*, and liberated resources from institutional spaces and moved them to community as often as I could. I've done more, but I shouldn't put it in writing (and neither should you, lesson one).

    May this letter find you grounded in community and living your values, even as your survival, your labor, and your basic needs are vilified, exploited, or criminalized. For some of us, these conditions are all too familiar. *For people organizing within the sex trades, or whose harm reduction work occurs outside the law, public scorn and carceral violence come with the territory.* As someone who has done (and continues to do) movement work within these spheres, I want to share some thoughts, and lessons I've learned, with people who are trying to do the work of collective survival in these environments. If you are not a sex worker or involved in harm reduction work, you may also have something to learn from people whose political work often occurs outside the law (or in direct opposition to it). As authoritarianism tightens its grip, more and more people are going to face criminalization upon choosing to organize as workers, resist unjust policies, or practice mutual aid. If you are grappling with the difficulties that come with this kind of work, here's what I can share . . .

I cannot stress enough how crucial it is to have a small, tight-knit crew you call your chosen political family. These can be people you actively organize with, or used to; or maybe you're all involved in different projects now; maybe you met at the club, clinic, or on the stroll; but these are your people who know you, trust you, are conflict brave, and can gut-check you. You've engaged in political education together, you have shared values, and you have experience—these are qualities that are earned and grown collectively. There are no substitutes for these kinds of relationships. Lots of people will tell you what to do; these are the people whose advice you should consider first and foremost.

That being said, *it is the criminality of the work that I need to focus on.* Or at least the impact of criminalization on our waged work, our organizing work—our political work (because all labor is politicized). Whether you're already accustomed to breaking the law, or you're just now finding yourself on the "wrong" side of the law (read as the *right side* of history), I hope this helps.

So you're an outlaw now? It was only a matter of time.

Unlearn the language of "good," "innocent," or "wrongfully." This is not just a rhetorical shift, but a shift in values. Let go of any preconceived notions you had about "criminals." In fact, let me officially welcome you to the criminal class. Divorcing oneself from respectability politics can be hard, especially when you're perceived as criminal or charged as such, and there are so many barriers to resources. There are no "good ones"; there are only people, fellow workers, co-strugglers. Innocence is irrelevant because the laws have already betrayed us. And it is my belief that no one should be caged, tortured, detained, or deported by the state—all carceral violence is unjustifiable. We cannot pick and choose who rightfully and wrongfully experiences the hell of carcerality. If we do this, we are affirming the very system that seeks to kill us.

You must commit to unapologetic politics. It might be tempting to give into something we call the *whorearchy*—or the hierarchical stratification of sex working/trading people whose perceived value or worth is ranked based upon the associated stigma of their particular form of sex work (i.e., "I'm better than them because I work indoors instead of on the street," or, "I don't deserve to be arrested because I'm paying for school, not drugs"). Whorearchy exists because of classism, colorism, substance stigma, racism, xenophobia, transmisogyny, ableism, and other forms of discriminatory, oppressive ideologies. But whorearchy *thrives* because of the criminalization and stigma of the sex trades. There are no shortcuts to liberation, and winning rights for some at the expense of others in our criminal class is a kind of soul death. When building a broad coalition, and involving people who have feminist and abolitionist politics, make sure you're not so quick to win them over that you abandon your lived experiences for the sake of *respectability*. Remember, those elites in power don't actually care if you pander to them now, if your existence threatens their agenda; they will never honor your humanity, no matter how "good" and "respectable" you try to be. Remain illegible and unruly.

Skill up as many people as you know, now. Your skill shares do not need to be large or public or perfect. They just need to happen thoughtfully, carefully, and often. Refreshing your own skill sets on gunshot-wound care, overdose reversal, rescue breathing, needle cleaning/disposal, learning the right quantities of misoprostol and mifepristone, and testing drugs for fentanyl and xylazine is a priority. Getting people together in person to build safer-sniffing kits, and to gather other harm reduction supplies, creates social community opportunities to check in on each other, engage in risk and movement assessments collectively, and share advice on using and caring for our comrades who use drugs. There is no substitute for offline, in-person conversations about strategy, tactics, and navigating work outside of the law.

The work is both urgent and patient. It is urgent in that these are timely skills that more of us need to learn and practice, especially since the majority of people will still call 9-1-1 even though they may be scared of the potential for police violence. Often this comes down to a lack of self-trust and lack of knowledge of how to intervene in an emergency situation without the state. When you're a sex worker and your client or fellow worker overdoses, you need to be able to act swiftly outside of the law whenever possible. Remember, you don't need to reinvent the wheel; radical harm reductionists and sex workers have been making tool kits, zines, and DIY guides for decades. Find what speaks to you and use it as a template; build on something that already exists and fact-check it with trusted friends. This work is patient because new skills may need to be acquired, because language and practices change with new knowledge, and because people will say some really upsetting and problematic shit to you about drug use. I'm so sorry, but they will—even the comrades who you think should know better. You can't see everyone's journey through; focus on the skills and recommit to a politics of solidarity and care. It's hard work doing peer-to-peer education: it can be draining, and you'll need to ask for help, a lot. Take a deep breath. You've got this.

Be discerning, and figure out who's in the room. There's practicing safer communication (what I used to call "security culture," before the term was wrecked and the concept debased), and then there's becoming obsessive and gatekeeping. What I'm expressly advocating, especially within criminalized workplace contexts, is moving things offline whenever possible. Learn how to assess risks as an individual within a formation, and collectively for the formation as a whole. Technology will change, adapt, and entrap. Work only with platforms that have clear terms of service and aren't already committed to throwing you under the bus, or expressly work with platforms that are built by community-minded people. Often, we can't control how we make money, or how platform consolidation will impact us and our work, both as activists and sex workers. But when it comes to our organizing work, we can opt in and out of using tools that don't serve us. We can also control what we do and don't say, and to who. This is critical—you have to move at the speed of trust. That will likely feel slower than you desire to act. You've got to get to a place where trust, collaboration, and safer outcomes for your communities are prioritized over optics and social media cred, jeopardizing your own safety to respond to every direct-service ask, or inflating your organization's numbers too rapidly.

Yes, the work will present new challenges, and there will be learning curves, but an emphasis on safer communication means talking regularly with the people with whom you are directly organizing—checking in on materials, assessing needs and risks, outlining safer methods to trade sex or obtain substances, discussing the political landscape in real terms, and making space to do visioning work beyond immediate crisis-related tasks. If you are doing work outside of the law, you cannot do this on a Zoom call with ninety-plus people you do not know. You also cannot do this at a large general-membership meeting of an organization that's open to the public. It will mean you have to repeat yourself, schedule more meetings, and develop an ear for infiltration. Some of these skills feel intuitive, but I promise, if you and your crew are paying attention, they can be learned, practiced, and modified for your own needs.

Sex workers, and really all workers in criminalized economies, have gotten really good at developing new languages, code-switching, and sharing information to keep each other safe by getting creative and working both within and against the repressive laws and their enforcement. You're being hoisted onto the shoulders of some tough, resourceful worker-organizers. You too will build and experiment with new tech, new skills, new tactics. Something that remains, however, is how you embody your politics and values. Don't let people shut sex workers and drug users out of spaces you find yourself working in—speak up, point to the outlaw legacies of harm reduction and mutual care, be bold in your comradeship.

Remember, you're not alone. Like Eugene V. Debs said, "While there is a lower class, I am in it, while there is a criminal element, I am of it, and while there is a soul in prison, I am not free."

Your co-conspirator,
Red

Brit "Red" Schulte is a community organizer, zine maker, doctoral candidate, and underemployed sex-working art historian. They helped organize the Justice for Alisha Walker Defense Campaign, transitioned Bluestockings Bookstore into a worker-owned cooperative, and are a founding member of the Support Ho(s)e Collective. Since the mid 2010s, they've organized with Hacking//Hustling, Survivors Against SESTA, Survived & Punished NY, Red Canary Song, and Slutwalk Chicago.

Read This if You've Been Assaulted (I Believe You)

Leanne Betasamosake Simpson

My Friend,

    I see you sitting there, alone, spreading out the shattered pieces, one by one. I want you to know that I believe you. I'm so sorry this happened to you. This is not your fault. You've done nothing wrong. Any shame you are feeling belongs to the person that did this to you, not to you.

    Whatever you are feeling is okay. You might feel very alone, but you're not alone because I'm here writing to you, and your ancestors and my ancestors are all around us, taking care. I'm here listening with only my heart. Without judgment.

    I know we want our organizing spaces to be free from gender and sexual violence, transphobia, and homophobia. Sometimes they are, and sometimes they are not. This is not a failure of you, or even of our movement spaces. We have been born into a settler colonial state, created by dispossessing Indigenous peoples of their lands, and by forcing our bodies and minds into hierarchy and gender binaries. We have been born into the slow genocide of the Americas and the tremendous violence of the afterlives of transatlantic slavery. Our relations and ancestors have faced this. Our comrades in Palestine and Sudan face this relentlessly. None of us are immune.

    The worst moments of my life have involved intimate violence. It has haunted my personal life since I was a child and relentlessly haunted my professional life as soon as I had one. I'm

Indigenous, and gender violence has been a constant tool colonizers have used to demobilize us. The residential school era infected us with an epidemic of assault, and most of us are survivors. I want more than anything for us to build worlds where this kind of violence is unthinkable, so no one has to go through what you are going through ever again. I know that's why we do this work.

These are difficult hours and difficult days.

When intimate violence happens in our own spaces, it can feel like all of our work and sacrifice and struggle is for nothing. If we can't embody our own values and treat each other with consent and respect, how can anything ever get better?! How can we face the harm these actions cause in a way that is transformative and still do the work we came together to do? How are there enough hours in the day to process everything we have to process?

Gender violence can bring down a collective or a movement or a family or just us, so quickly. Given the pervasiveness of these types of violence in our society, the onus is on movement spaces and collectives to learn how to respond to a survivor's bravery with support and care. The most recent time I was dealing with intimate violence, my community surrounded me with support and care. I was believed. I was offered time off. I had the resources to find a trauma therapist for three months of weekly meetings. I was encouraged to stay in my own experience and focus on my own needs and self-determination.

There is a difference between how we write, organize, and theorize about gender violence and what it feels like to experience it. Sometimes we can't understand or believe how, knowing what we know, we could get caught up in it. Sometimes we need someone to remind us that the colonizers infused the air with intimate violence, and we do what we can to see it, resist it, and transform it. This isn't your fault. You don't have to worry about the movement or the collective right now. You just need to take care of you.

I want to make sure you're supported. Do you have someone you trust with whom you can talk? These friends are not always easy to find, because sometimes the ones closest to us are de-skilled in assisting those of us that are recovering from sexual assault. I took a very haphazard approach to this. I told a lot of people, then watched how they responded. What I learned is that those people in my life who were good at taking care of me when I was sick or depressed were also good in this situation. Those that meant well but distanced themselves, centered themselves, or were triggered by their own unprocessed trauma still loved and cared about me but did not have the skills to support my healing, and I required boundaries in our relationship to keep myself safe. For this group, I assigned tasks like making food and taking over work responsibilities. Is there someone who can make you tea or food? Is there someone in your crew who can organize a pod of hearts around you to support you in the days and months ahead?

You should know that I'm not an expert on this, but that there are people who can help in important ways. Do you need to get medical care? Who can go with you? Do you want to talk with a therapist? Can someone help you find supports for survivors in your area? There are lots of options, and you're in charge. What was helpful to me was learning about trauma and how my body, mind, and spirit were processing it. With a therapist, I learned what was happening to my body and my mind both in the moment and in the months afterward. I learned simple ways to support my body's healing process. I learned why I was hypervigilant and panicking in crowds. I learned that simply lying on my back and putting my feet up the wall helped my nervous system calm down. I learned about breathing and somatic exercises. I learned how to help my body into feeling safe.

What are the things you need right now, in this moment?

I shudder when people ask me that question, because I never know what I need. I need friends to suggest basic things like drinking water and eating sandwiches and putting on lip balm. Or things like showering and going outside to find sunlight. Walking a little bit, or maybe stretching my back, or listening to just one song, or the sound of waves.

Sometimes tiny things help in tiny ways.

It's okay to step back from the work and from your regular responsibilities. It's okay to take the time you need to gather and ground yourself. And it is also okay to continue on. Everyone processes differently and on their own time frame.

Remember to love yourself extra and to be your own very best friend. Breathe deep, rhythmic breaths for a few minutes. Stretch. Walk. Run. Find ways to reset your nervous system. Feel all your feelings. Remember, you are good and perfect just the way you are. Paint or write poetry. Writing helps me because it gives me (back) my voice. Creative practice always helps me find my way through.

This is not your fault. None of it.

Remember, it's not your responsibility to fix this or make other people feel comfortable or do the right thing. Your only responsibility, right now, is to you.

Remember that even when you feel alone, you are part of a forest of living things that care deeply about you and your well-being. We are all connected. You are an important hub in our web.

Remember that water heals. Tiny, tiny bits at a time that you don't notice. Water keeps at it, though, and over time it carves banks and holes out of rock.

I see your light and the embers of your fire, still glowing. Think about what you can do to stoke those embers and grow your flames.

Sending you love and strength,
Leanne Betasamosake Simpson

Leanne Betasamosake Simpson is a Michi Saagiig Nishnaabeg writer, musician, intellectual, and member of Alderville First Nation. She is the author of nine books including *Rehearsals for Living* (coauthored with Robyn Maynard; Haymarket Books, 2022), and *Theory of Water: Nishnaabe Maps to the Times Ahead* (Haymarket Books, 2025).

Read This if You're a Parent Feeling Isolated
Atena Danner

Dear Co-struggling Parent,

    I was a thirty-year-old mother of two when the Occupy movement launched. That month, I was sitting in a restaurant in Chicago's Lincoln Square neighborhood having a committee meeting over dinner with folks from my Unitarian Universalist church. They were nice, middle-class people—very feed-the-homeless, give-to-charity, liberal-and-proud folks. As we talked, someone started sharing news alerts about how young people were taking to the streets of downtown Chicago, facing off with the authorities in solidarity with the Occupy protests we'd heard about in New York City. Occupy Chicago was happening! My imagination flickered to life as visions of the marches and protests from my younger days flashed through my mind. One member of our group, a woman perhaps twenty years my senior, said, "I want to join them. I should be there." My heart raced as I sat quietly, feeling defeated as she spoke the sentiment I couldn't bring myself to express. I was mom to a toddler and a kindergartner at the time, and I did not feel safe heading to the encampments alone, fearing the possibility of arrest or violence. I didn't know anyone who would be there, and I was certain my then-partner would not be supportive. So I swallowed my desire to jump into action. As the conversation eventually returned to committee work, deep yearning enveloped me, my thoughts stuck on Occupy. I was alone in that moment, in a cocoon of my own unmet need. It would take me years before I could successfully reconcile my desire to join actions with the overwhelming responsibilities of parenting, but I was able to get there eventually with the support of a community of radical co-strugglers that 2011 Atena could scarcely imagine.

If You Are Feeling Disengaged

Caring for children is tough as fuck in the best of circumstances. But you are not alone. The demands of being a parent can be very challenging for anyone who wants to be involved in organizing and activism. If you are an organizer or activist who is newer to parenting, or a parent who is embarking on a new organizing journey, this is written with deep love and solidarity, especially for you. (If you are not that parent, or not a parent at all, you should still read these words; they are relevant to anyone who wants their movement building to last beyond their own generation.)

The lessons I have learned as a caregiver who wants to organize for a better world basically amount to some version of the following: to be a successful organizer/activist or parent, you will not get far without the core elements of community and care. Barriers to those experiencing those core elements are baked into our dysfunctional society, so we have to be intentional about overcoming them and vigilantly keep them at bay.

There are many ways of being a caregiver. My orientation as a queer Black woman with Black kids colors how I approach this whole thing. I am a divorced person coparenting teens with both an ex-partner and my current partner, and the genders / gender roles are all over the place (I call this arrangement Modern Fucking Family). I have seen caregiving manifest in beautiful poly-parent situations, family-as-neighbor homes, neighbor-as-family care, aunties-as-extra-moms families, and siblings-take-turns-sitting-with-elder-Mama. All are valid and necessary—the more families we can imagine, the wider the web we can create. As climate change becomes more pronounced and systems we rely on get shaken up, we are gonna need each other in all our glorious formations.

When I became a parent, I was not engaged in any hands-on activism. I ended my first year of graduate school in late July 2005 and gave birth in September to a beautiful baby with spina bifida. While the baby was rushed off to a separate children's hospital mere hours after their birth to undergo spinal surgery, I stayed in my hospital to recover from the C-section. I credit my midwife Sarah with making sure I was able to at least touch my baby before they were taken away because I wouldn't see them for three very long days; Sarah made sure I was able to provide that small act of care before our separation—my first post-pregnancy act of care. When we were reunited, I was only able to hold them for a few minutes at a time for the next couple of weeks, and as the chill of fall weather set in outside, I spent most of my time in the neonatal intensive care unit pumping and thickening breast milk, dressing the baby's surgery wound, caring for my own surgery wound, changing diapers, and drifting, shell-shocked, through Children's Memorial in my gray bathrobe: a mom-shaped shadow that only materialized into flesh when I was with my baby. I take the time to share these details of care because care matters. Individual acts of care matter, and over time acts of care accumulate to provide an antidote to the isolation that frequently troubles caregivers, as well as a reserve of positive feelings that fortifies our well-being and resilience.

That was nineteen years ago. Between then and now, it took years for me to do anything besides keep a very small person alive. When my firstborn was older, I attempted some organizing within my church community, but, having had a second baby, three and a half years after the first, I became very overwhelmed. My eldest was nine years old before I got into any sustainable activism. If you are in some version of this place on your parenting journey, I want to make sure that you know: YOU ARE DOING ENOUGH. KEEPING ANOTHER HUMAN ALIVE IS ENOUGH. Even if you're not in the hospital, not chestfeeding, or have plenty of parental leave. Even if you have older kiddos—whatever. This shit is hard.

If You're Feeling the Not-Enoughness

Our feelings of inadequacy are not accidental or unique. Cishet, patriarchal, misogynist, ableist, white supremacist, capitalist, xenophobic, colonial, racist society makes it incredibly difficult for any of us to provide optimal levels of care necessary for healthy development of human animals with souls and soft needs. Every element and complex intersection within these constellations of oppression works to break us down and use our resources to fuel its own survival. Resisting those systems while caring for dependents is like enduring the Hunger Games with a child strapped to your body. It's not a fair fight, and the best way to win is to team up with folks who will mutually protect and fight with each other, bust out of the arena, and shut down the whole fucking game. The limitations created by oppression make us feel like we're never doing as much as we should be, however hard we might try.

As a parent of high-impact, neurodivergent, and disabled kiddos—a parent who works full time, volunteers, and makes art when I can—there have been many times I've needed to tell myself not to measure my actions against the metrics of other people's lives. Now, I'm able to catch those thoughts early and show them the door, recognizing the lie as a conspiracy between capitalist hustle culture and societal over-reliance on the labor of those who are already doing too much (including Black and Brown women, femmes doing protective and self-defense work, familial and community caregivers, cash-strapped folks, emotional labor load-carriers, and so on). Instead of dehumanizing each other with comparisons and imposed stories, let's start being honest about the impermanent and conditional nature of capacity.

The trick of "enough"—as in "not good enough," "not trying

hard enough," "not doing enough"—is one of the dirtiest, trickiest, sneakiest traps that any of us can get caught up in. We were all set up, brainwashed, and betrayed; *enough* is a lie. Every form of oppression and marginalization sings a pernicious whisper song of "not good enough!" that loops through our lives, day in and day out; parents and others who tend to carry the yoke of society's demands for service or performance are highly susceptible, but this gremlin of insecurity comes for us all, caregiver or otherwise. When we are personally responsible for the well-being of others, the whisper can tend to rise to full volume. It is one of the most insistent lies you will ever hear. Listen for that whisper, learn what it sounds like, and tell it to fuck right off.

Enough is also a paradox. The world suffers enormously; the best you can do will always be *enough* and simultaneously never *enough*. You always have the potential to make an impact, *and* your efforts will always need to be joined with the work of others. I say this to offer some relief and/or hope; you can't win the game of *enough*, and you don't need to, because you've already won.

If You're Feeling Disconnected

In my journey as a parent, I've learned firsthand that it's possible—and sometimes easy—to become detached from yourself. My parents were involved in political activism and creative cultural organizing, which I participated in as a child and was raised to value. I lost touch with those values in my first marriage, where I slowly became isolated, further removed from the connections that reminded me what was important. This is something that can happen to us in a variety of unbalanced circumstances: out-of-whack work/life boundaries, inequitable partnerships, and even (often) parenting. When I prioritized the values of my partner over my own and afforded more care to my children than I expected for myself, I lost contact with what anchored me to my own values and identity.

If you are feeling that loss right now, I am sorry. It is such a hard place to be. It can be so hard to imagine that things could change for the better, but I hope you believe me when I say that with help, we can often find a healing path back to ourselves; connection is a major ingredient of the salve for this wound. One of my paths to healing started with reconnecting, during my unhappy marriage, with some old friends from art school. My friends Anita, Alica, and I gathered for a weeklong vacation at the end of 2012, and at that point, when I couldn't envision how to create a happier life, they poured care into me and treated me like the friend they had always known. It helped me begin 2013 with a reactivated connection to myself. When I returned home, I started looking for a way out of my unhappy situation. The care of friends helped me clear out the cobwebs and imagine a way forward. Two years later, I was blocking traffic as an action deployed around the International Association of Chiefs of Police Conference in Chicago. Care facilitates growth and transformation. Who pours care into you?

Sometimes parenting sucks; it's hard, and often we don't know what we're doing and have to do it anyway, hoping we don't ruin a human. The stress of these stakes is incredible. Our multiply oppressive society complicates all of these wounds and makes parenting even more difficult—at times, seemingly impossible. When we manage to heal wounds by thwarting isolation and affirming our selfhood, it frees up energy and breaks down barriers, making it possible to hear and answer the call to liberation work.

If You Are Feeling Isolated

My theory is that for people experiencing oppression, barriers tend to amount to wounds, and their solutions come from healing. When we recognize the wound, we have a better shot at healing. In parenting, the wound is often loss of personal identity and social displacement. This crystalized for me years ago, during a party at a friend's house. Most of the guests were sitting at a table together chatting, drinking, and laughing. My friend and I found ourselves on the floor on the other side of the room, entertaining the nursing toddlers. The other adults stopped looking at us or talking to us, as if an invisible screen had been placed between us. As young adults who had been pulled away from our familiar social networks by the demands of parenting, we were excited to reengage in spaces where we had previously belonged but found that we were suddenly invisible in those spaces: a painful blow to anyone's sense of identity. The medicine for loss of identity is reengagement of culture, connection with people who light a path for us back to ourselves, and community building. The medicine for social displacement is the same, with special attention to belonging. My friend Pura Verdad speaks to this, noting that to do social justice and liberation work, she needs a sense of "feeling safe to be, safe to bring 'lils,' [and] being appreciated."

Activist spaces are often structured in ways that favor quick mobility and overwork—to the detriment of access. This can run counter to the needs of parents of young children in particular, and tends to indicate unexamined ableism. Thankfully, due to the growing prevalence of conversations about boundaries, access, community care, and rest, more and more people in movement spaces are figuring out how to value a diversity of approaches, paces, and levels of access. Spaces that are intentional about access have always been easiest for me to participate in as a parent. When organizers are planning for disability access, they sometimes end up addressing shared needs of parents and children: bathroom access, seating and rest areas, wheel-friendly travel ways, and extra time for transitions, to name a few.

Isolation and loneliness are huge contributors to the vicious cycle of being unmotivated and uninvolved. We're social creatures. We need to know that someone cares about us—someone who will help us figure out whether we're getting things right, and help us notice if we're off track. Isolated parents can be tempted to get this from our own kids. However, it would be a mistake to tie our identity and self-worth to our kiddos: they are whole human beings, and they have the right to be the center of their own universes while they navigate How to Be a Person 101. This is why we need other organizer and activist parents in our lives. They are the ones who can relate to this particular brand of identity loss and need for affirmation. Experienced movement parents can help us negotiate the added layers of time management and energy budgeting that come with caregiving. Those connections that serve as guides and supports on your journey to incorporate social justice work can be lifesavers! They can also help us reset our barometers if our expectations become out of whack with reality.

If You're Feeling Excluded

I've never enjoyed feeling excluded as a parent—but experiencing exclusion can become a way to identify key qualities you are seeking in an organizing community. For example, do you see respect for children and families in the space? Do you find that the values and energies in the organizing match what you and your family need?

One barrier to involvement I've faced is finding organizing communities that truly accommodate children, especially when they're hungry, tired, or cranky. As parents, we learn just how wildly energy levels for kids and parents can vary. Kids often need more rest and food than adults, and they are more likely to melt down if their needs are not promptly met. Sometimes we have to tap out if they are at the end of their rope. This can be disappointing, especially when it means we'll miss out on gatherings where wins are celebrated, or losses commiserated. When comrades recognize this and plan accordingly, it combats those feelings of exclusion and makes it easier to stay engaged. Another Chicago parent-organizer, Halle Frances Quezada Rasmussen, describes how multigenerational inclusion helps her stay involved:

"If I can bring my kids with me and they're actually welcomed . . . it helps them feel like they are supposed to be there too." There's nothing like when folks are able to anticipate ways to support us! There have been people who would have made space for me to pump milk or change diapers if I'd explained, but I was often so tired of providing models for my own consideration that I'd sometimes choose to sit it out and stay home with my short-fuse bladder and leaky boobs. No one can be expected to read minds, but anyone can be curious about who isn't at the table and what can be done to bring us in.

Barriers to our involvement can involve simple factors that, once identified, are in fact easy to overcome. When my older kid was a toddler, I traveled to a social justice conference for Unitarian Universalist young adults. I was encouraged to bring the baby, and in many ways it was a wonderful time! People were so welcoming, and there were a few other parents there too. I was traveling with a friend: a parent of a similar-aged child who was willing to take turns nursing the little ones, showering, and grabbing trays of food for each other. This collaboration made travel seem possible in a way that it hadn't before. However, I'll never forget how our first meeting space was a room over-crowded with furniture and other assorted junk with a filthy floor; there was no clean, hazard-free space where I could just put my toddler down for a couple of minutes. I was exhausted from holding on to a very energetic person who was determined to explore that crowded, dirty space. It hadn't occurred to me to ask for a childproofed meeting space with a clean floor, and the organizers hadn't known why that would be important; they hadn't realized that conditions adults can easily ignore can be unsafe for small children. This is not a matter of blaming anyone but of making our labor visible; people need to be aware that effort required to mitigate risk to the child usually falls on the parent, and the cost is our energy.

Our family has had a few experiences where access and inclusion were incorporated with greater intention than usual, which made bringing children along significantly easier. Spaces that stand out include the childcare spaces at Allied Media Conference in 2015, and WisCon (a progressive speculative fiction convention that takes place annually in Wisconsin) in 2017. In both situations, the volunteers approached caring for youth with respect, curiosity, and consideration of their ages and stages. The kids were offered planned activities and appropriately structured time. These alignments should inform our plans for inclusive futures and prompt the question: How else can we use care to widen the circle?

When on a low battery after the tiring work of caregiving (while swimming upstream against capitalism, heteronormativity, et al.), our response to the idea of self-advocating and supervising our own inclusion is often a big, juicy "NOPE." While these misalignments can be frustrating, we can and should learn from them. I find it best to avoid judgment about the persistent tensions that often exist between parents and child-free folks; templates designed by misogyny, capitalist patriarchy, and ableism feed the separation and exclusion between these groups. Both groups may experience benefits and privileges desired by the other, and both are shamed away from admiring or desiring what the other has. A mother who wants to move around unencumbered by her children is considered selfish and may be rewarded socially if she suppresses that want to model an archetype of selfless motherhood. A masculine child-free person who expresses interest in parenting is often considered odd at best, suspect at worst, and will instead be rewarded for eschewing nurturing care for violence and misogyny. To create a society where shame, sexism, and violence are not the prevailing values, we need diverse models of care, support, connection, and community building. Our work for better health care, better access to quality education, and more sustainable systems for using and distributing survival resources are endangered when we are caught in cycles of criticism and judgment.

Have you ever encountered people who behave as though indifference or condescension toward children are undetectable behaviors? It's never made me feel welcome. I'm not motivated to return to spaces where folks are disrespectful or unkind in their eagerness to explain why they are choosing not to parent. To those people I say: I wish you peace, and I hope we can engage in the struggle together. I empathize with the hurt that causes people to over-defend their choice to remain child free. We all have our own gender-based or reproductive *injustice* wounds to heal; often they are generational wounds. I can see how sharing space with parents and children might activate those hurts. Still, if need be, we may need to gently remind them: neither our kids or us are responsible for your feelings, and we expect to be treated with respect.

If You Don't Know Where to Start

When I got back into activism, I was a single mother of two elementary school kids and had been working in the field of early childhood education. A good friend that I trust brought the Chicago Childcare Collective (Chichico) to my attention, knowing that it aligned with my knowledge and skills as well as my need for a kid-friendly environment. Many people in the group were in relationship with friends of mine or part of familiar activist circles. As a new and wary organizer-parent, connecting with people I could trust was essential. I started showing up when and where I was able, and soon I was developing connections with parents and with a significant number of child-free co-strugglers.

Chichico included some of the raddest organizers I'd ever met, and their inclusion of parents in social change activities had a major impact on what I expect from child-free organizers. I entered activist childcare with an established understanding that children and their families should be involved in social change work; I'd worked with doulas to organize pregnancy and birth-education events, and there was always some combination of parents, pregnant people, playing children, and nursing babies at our gatherings. I knew we could create that for each other; I had not known how beautifully comrades without kids could show up for parents and kiddos alike. Learning that parents have more than each other to rely on cracked my imagination open to let in so much light! Logistics like bedtime and school pickup were normal considerations when we planned events. Snacks and art supplies were the standard, and parent access to organizing spaces was prioritized. I'd written off a huge group of potential friends and comrades because of previous experiences of exclusion. I've since learned to raise my expectations and level-set early about what I need.

When our responsibilities as parents present barriers to joining social justice struggles, it can be overwhelming. We see activism represented in the media through imagery of crowded marches, riots, arrests, and the like. But media depictions seldom tell the full story; they are usually sensationalized and curated for certain agendas. When you find yourself at odds with the state or policymakers, it makes total sense to wonder, "What could happen to me and/or my kids?" Reasonable question. One of the first direct actions I was invited to join introduced me to the concept of green, yellow, and red roles for participants. If I had parenting time the next day, I could identify a green role to fulfill: what a relief! This kind of structure meant I didn't have to assume that signing up for direct action meant signing up for arrest. Comrades explained that I could choose how and when to engage (with the understanding that there's always some risk), and we made specific plans to keep each other safe. These assurances of care made it possible for me to support causes with more confidence.

As you examine opportunities to get involved with activism, remember to ask yourself, "What is possible?" "Who is out there ready to welcome me/us?" Find someone to share your fears with who will help you approach them with curiosity, and from a place of care. Start by talking to other parents and organizers: Do they know about any local parent-organizing efforts, or childcare collectives? Who is already doing work that is important to you? Have they already made space for family considerations, or are they open to learning? Somewhere, someone is willing to address your concerns, to move a meeting time or push for a location with a kid-friendly space if it means you'll be there. There is a place for you. Every investment we make in care and community adds to the story of how we win, including who we do this work with and how we treat each other. That is what the kiddos see when we don't know they're looking, and it fuels the memories they draw on when the world is in their hands. The belonging we find in values-aligned community makes organizing and activism more sustainable. For me, Chicago Childcare Collective supported the recovery of my identity as an activist and organizer because the values demonstrated within the collective were ones that I wanted to strengthen in myself, and that I wanted my children to carry into the future. My childcare collective comrades' approach of normalized family inclusion removed the barrier of isolation, and their radically inclusive respect for children's intellect and agency fostered a sense of belonging for my family. My initiation into Chichico's radical care work helped me reimagine how caregivers and young people might hold and activate our power to make social change. It bolstered my willingness to clarify my needs and honor my boundaries as a parent. I began to be less self-conscious about having my children with me, and more vocal about resisting child segregation when working to create space for caregivers. If we can reach toward our kid-free comrades and they can meet us with curiosity and care, we can start building authentic intergenerational spaces for co-learning and action.

There will be times when our doubt eclipses our resources. These times are an opportunity to reconnect with our values and commitments. When things are hardest, experience has taught me to slow down, get grounded in my senses, and seek connection with people who will remind me who the fuck I am. Refill your tank of affirming connections early and often. Our children tend to follow what they see much more often than what we say, and that includes how we solve problems, approach conflict, and care for ourselves.

I often think about the world I want my children to inherit. It breaks my heart how the promise of that world falls further and further away from us as the logical consequences of unceasing profit expansion, callous dehumanization, and reckless environmental abuse rage across our lands, skies, and waters. As much as I hate to admit it, bad things have been planted, and my babies will have to reap that harvest. Organizing and activism are how I try to stem the tide of terrible outcomes, even as people with more resources are determined to drive us full throttle into a metaphorical brick wall. I hope that the rising generations will wrest control of this vessel from them and find a way to recover a livable planet for humanity. This is why a part of me always appreciates my children's defiance, even when it enrages me; I brought them into a world on a radically different trajectory than I was prepared for. These kids have to survive in a future that I can barely imagine. To solve for the impending terrible things, they have to be primed for resistance, ready to push back against limited imaginations—even mine.

Parenting demonstrates that the *how* of our actions is as important as the *what* and *why*. As people who are responsible for children, it is our duty not only to win our battles and create the best conditions possible, but also to show subsequent generations how to move purposefully and with care: to show them how collective care weakens oppression and strengthens our communities. Acknowledging community care as an essential element of collective liberation challenges the culture of parental self-sacrifice, a toxic culture whose reinforcement serves only to teach our children to sacrifice themselves. We must envision our children living in their future—yes!—*and* we must remember to see ourselves: we are the experienced weavers who hold the stories of humanity. I appreciate the wisdom of my friend Holly Krig, who once said, "I know that if we are not part of this work, supported in doing this work, we not only risk losing a generation of organizers—but we lose the people who share a commitment to mutual care as central to the work, as well as all the skills we must learn to navigate and challenge divestment and other 'ordinary' violence." While we prepare to eventually hand things over, we still have to travel alongside the young ones for a while. It would be a mistake to ignore the next generation and deprive them of the hard-won lessons of our inherited struggles. It would also be a mistake to treat ourselves as though we are already gone and no longer essential. Each of us is an important part of the larger interdependent whole: not cogs in a machine but stars in the cosmic web, interconnected by gravity and endless lessons. Let's make our way forward together in solidarity, taking good care of ourselves and each other, and teaching our young ones to weave our stories of care into the future.

Your comrade,
Atena

Atena O. Danner is a cultural worker who imagines Black liberation, engaged in boundless curiosity. As a poet, singer, and visual artist, Atena creates work that encompasses kitchen-table specificity and folk story relatability, covering topics including neurodiversity, human connection, and collective liberation. As an organizer and activist, she has worked to incorporate struggles for justice into her life as a caregiver in a family of complex needs while also writing and publishing in journals, anthologies, and her own book of poetry, *Incantations for Rest: Poems, Meditations & Other Magic* (Skinner House, 2022), which was awarded a Nautilus Silver Award for poetry in 2023.

Read This if You Are Panicking about Collapse
Chris Begley

Dear Reader,

 I'll get right to the point: I understand the sentiment that we are rearranging deck chairs on the *Titanic*. Aren't we on a sinking ship? Should not all our efforts be directed toward stopping the sinking that is climate change and ecological destruction? If we can't, why bother with any of the things on which we spend our energy? Can we worry about beauty, truth, or justice while fighting for our lives, or the life of our planet? Many of us whose work does not focus on immediate needs have struggled to reconcile this. I have asked these same questions.

 Let me tell you how I navigate those doubts and questions, and why I think your efforts are not futile. In fact, I think they are more important now than ever. We need people to point out when things are not fair, and to help make our world equitable. We need artists and scholars to help us understand what we are going through.

 We can start with the laws of physics. Entropy. Everything falls apart—that's a given. None of this lasts forever, and we know that. We do not look at a child and ask, "What's the point? Why educate them? Why feed them? They are just going to die someday." That scenario is ridiculous. We routinely invest in things that will not last forever.

 Since nothing is permanent, how close to the end do you need to be for it not to be worth it anymore? We try to minimize the suffering of people or animals, even at the very ends of their lives. We do not need permanence to make something valuable. We live in the present, always, and if there is a present, things matter. What you do matters now, and even if that was all we had, that is enough.

Maybe at this point I should object to my own metaphor. You are not rearranging deck chairs. You are doing important, significant things, as are so many others: creating a just society, safeguarding pieces of the world around us, preserving our connections to our history, easing suffering, educating, informing, questioning, protesting, demanding change, creating beauty, or acknowledging somebody else's reality. None of that is trivial. Being part of a family or community and working to improve it for everybody—that, by itself, is worth the effort, no matter what is on the horizon.

I am an archaeologist, which means I study how things fall apart. From looking at many examples of collapsing civilizations, I see some common themes that can help us understand what we are facing, and how others have faced it before us.

Civilizations fall apart all the time, and it almost always takes a long time. Entire lives are lived during some societal collapses. Sometimes, the collapse can span generations. Those people and those communities matter. They created meaningful lives during a larger disaster. Even if we are in the midst of a societal collapse, the needs remain. We need the bulwarks against injustice, ignorance, and cruelty; we will need you. In fact, the need may be greater than ever, since tough times do not always bring out the best in us.

Another thing we see looking back in time is that great transformations affect different groups in very different ways; their impacts are not uniform. Falling apart looks different from other perspectives and happens at different rates. By the time some of us realize things are changing, and that a disaster is upon us, others of us will have been living with that reality for some time. Where I live, climate change has only recently produced dramatic events that make it clear what is happening. In other parts of the world, people have seen disastrous changes for decades. Is it pointless to continue working on our communities now that we see clearly what others have seen for a long time?

I keep using the word "community" for a reason. Looking at past catastrophes, we see that people survive as a community, not individuals. We survive as a collective, and we have a role and responsibilities as members of a community. It will be social and political skills that allow us to make it through. How we treat people matters. Generosity, fairness, and empathy are not just favors to others; they are how we create the community in which we must live. When everyone is allowed to contribute, we all benefit.

Our actions might seem esoteric, or nonessential, but they can impact the entire group—maybe inspire the group. Maybe those actions inspire people or expand our vision for our collective future. Where we are heading is not predetermined or inflexible—our actions steer us into the future. Anything we do to improve our situation now can be used to create a new reality, or to improve on one in which we find ourselves. The work is never done, and may seem insignificant in the scheme of things, but it can and will transform our reality going forward. Could the ship be sinking because injustice or ignorance or cruelty keeps us from seeing a solution? What if our efforts to improve our community in the present can help us find ways to keep it from going under? Think of all the brilliant minds that do not have the luxury of looking beyond daily struggles for food, shelter, safety, or dignity. What if those minds were freed up? What could they accomplish, and how could that change our destiny? The most important survival skills are not how to start a fire or build a shelter, but how to create and maintain a community.

We imagine how the future will look. We know some truths about the future, but we can't know precisely how everything will play out. We can't start ignoring the present because of an image of the future that seems hopeless, for that vision is undoubtedly simplistic and one-dimensional compared to the future in which we will live.

Maybe all of this misses a fundamental point: Why, in any case, would you stop doing what you do? After all, you don't do this work for reward or recognition but because it's the right thing to do, and because it matters. In moments of frustration, we often ask ourselves if it's worth it, and we decide it is. Strategies change, or the scale, or other particulars, but the work you do is not fragile, nor is its meaning so contingent on a particular situation that a change renders it unimportant. Let's take the example of something that does not directly address an immediate need: an artist creating discomfort, doubt, or beauty, or a scholar analyzing that art, or an archaeologist trying to preserve it for the future. None of that is only about the particular objects created, under study, or being preserved. What all of those people are doing goes far beyond the objects that are part of their current activities. They are seeking to understand something on a fundamental level, about ourselves or our community. The meaning in what they do is not fragile, not contingent, and not going to disappear. You know what you do matters, so keep it up. If everything is falling apart, we will all need more help, reflection, education, and challenges to our baser natures—not less.

Finally, let me mention something that you might not see in yourself. You, your actions, investing in your community, sends a message and can change the future. This is true now, and it will be doubly true when things get worse. By providing an example of somebody who still cares, who still works, you never know who you might inspire or what change you might help bring about. Be that example. Keep being that example.

Sincerely,
Chris

Chris Begley is a maritime archaeologist, writer, and journalist. He has a doctorate from the University of Chicago, was a Fulbright Scholar, and is a National Geographic Explorer. He is the author of *The Next Apocalypse: The Art and Science of Survival* (Basic Books, 2021).

Read This if You Want to Defeat Fascism

Shane Burley

Dear Comrade,

You know as well as I know that revolution is simply impossible when fascism is ascendant.

You are likely reading this because you are looking for a pathway not just out of our seemingly intractable present but into a more humane future. We are forced to conceive of politics primarily through our modern electoral system, a process where our sense of the possible is whittled down so completely that scarcely any window into a liberated world remains. When we step more fully into our imagination, when we walk away from the narrow bounds we are provided to contain our dreams, that is when a brief picture of revolution becomes available.

How do we get to a world where difference and identity is celebrated? Where the earth returns to the center of life, healed and thriving, with balance and stability? Where labor becomes the product of joy and our want and need is simply expressed through our passions to grow even greater, together? This kind of society is so foreign that it feels like an exercise in literary genre, what you would write if you had complete freedom to write what you wanted on the page. But this is exactly the type of project in which radical politics invites you to join. Radicalism as such is founded on a *breaking* moment, a shattering of our current structures by force of cataclysm. And if we want to bust out of even the fruitless upheavals, uprisings that feel prescient and yet, ultimately, lead to more of the same, we need a revolution like none other.

Revolutions do not materialize simply by force of popular will but rely on material conditions and, to a degree, the contradictions of everyday immiseration. Revolutions occur when they *can* happen, when discontent has accelerated from simmering to a boil, when institutions teeter, and when enough people have a shared experience of disempowerment that they can use this as the fulcrum point to build an unprecedented type of unity.

And this is also fascism's entry point: it takes that energy and uses it to snuff out our dreams.

Acknowledgment of this fact is one of the first steps with which any organizer on the radical left must grapple if they are to achieve any of the steppingstones on the way to that imaginative framework. A false assumption abounds that all organizers share the same lingo, vision, or even a consensus sense of the necessary tools involved. This letter is for everyone engaged actively in on-the-ground struggle but unsure what a swelling fascist threat looks like and exactly what kind of victim it can make of us. No matter what project you are a part of, what community you feel held by, what strategies you think will work and accomplices you believe you have, antifascism is required. Antifascism is the starting point because if our enemies win, they will take our new world in utero with them. Nothing is possible without it.

Fascist movements are built by capturing the frothing discontent of particular segments of the working class and contorting its sites away from the powerful and onto marginalized communities, confusing where oppression comes from, and, ultimately, defending the ruling class. On the left, economic and social instability are viewed as barriers to human dignity and liberation. Fascism feeds on this same precarity, infusing it with what philosopher Baruch Spinoza named "sad passions," such as desperate loneliness or envy, to create a manipulative emotional language about how it will alleviate our suffering.

There is a lot of discussion about a current political "realignment" taking place—mostly about how the right has changed. But it's happening among liberals as well. As crisis becomes undeniable, as consumer capitalism begins to sputter, and desolation and political volatility leads to crumbling civic institutions, the political center has utterly collapsed. The right has adopted national populist language and is speaking the language of revolution, a type that channels class consciousness into nationalism. But even while mutating the cause and solution, the right still acknowledges the state of the crisis. Establishment liberals have, instead, moved to the center, hoping to capture the elements of the right that miss the stasis of the 1990s and instead speak to oppression by simply painting a mural of diversity atop their machine of neoliberal trade and global exploitation. This dynamic reveals one of the most volatile threats that fascism holds: that it will appropriate the language of revolutionary upheaval, thus capturing a rank and file who simply will no longer accept the American mythology offered to them by the progressive intelligentsia, cultural institutions, or the Democratic Party.

The second, more glaringly obvious threat of a rising fascist force is its ability to enact unbelievable devastation on those it identifies as its primary enemies. Marginalized communities, the working class, and the left (by whom I mean the organized effort to advance the interest of the masses) are those against whom fascists ultimately have their guns drawn, and their success depends on our failure. We are not waiting for a revolution to begin; we are years in at this point, and the real question is what kind of society comes next. When we look at the histories of revolutions, we often forget that they often contain a civil war as well, a "three-way fight" that includes state and capital on one side and the fascists on the other.[1] The American empire and the fascist insurgency are not always one and the same (though they share key interests

---

1. See Xtn Alexander and Matthew N. Lyons, eds., *Three Way Fight: Revolutionary Politics and Antifascism* (Oakland: PM Press and Kersblebedeb, 2024).

and voices), but they are both in play as we fight out what type of world comes out the other side of capitalism's explosive evolution. As antifascist scholar Devin Zane Shaw writes, "Far-right movements are system-loyal when they perceive that the entitlements of white supremacy can be advanced within bourgeois or democratic institutions and they become insurgent when they perceive that these entitlements cannot."[2] Antifascists do not carry out this revolution in isolation; it is, rather, the result of successful interlocking social movements that take on every aspect of life, from labor to housing to the prison industrial complex, but antifascists are the wedge that protect them from assault and infiltration.

The Left's Challenge

The erosion of the liberal status quo, particularly the welfare state and the slow march of egalitarian social policies marking government policy, comes from the fact that our culture now expects revolution rather than reform. Even as the right runs a program to reshape the democratic state, it adopts the language of revolution, while the liberal center, what is called the left in the United States and many parts of Europe, uses the jargon of academia to offer up global trade by falsely suggesting it has egalitarian implications. The only option is to create a left whose vision of equality, on issues of both class and identity, are built directly on material resources, victories that can be measured, and the strength of solidarity. You build a united movement by showing every community, from blue-collar workers in the Rust Belt to those fighting desperately for access to lifesaving trans health care, that they are in the same fight and that their success and safety is bound up with that of one another. The denial of the slow destruction

---

2. Devin Zane Shaw, "Seven Theses on the Three-Way Fight," *Three Way Fight*, August 2, 2021, https://threewayfight.org/seven-theses-on-the-three-way-fight.

of consumer capitalism, the astounding collapse of basic social systems and services, and the institutionalization of cruelty as the national ethos will not build the militant alternative necessary to fight back the fascist recalibration of struggle. When people know something is terribly wrong in their lives, they simply won't trust those who think tax credits and means-tested vouchers will fix it. They would rather burn it down. And because of this central impulse, many confuse the methods with the results: when the world around you is on fire, it makes sense to choose violence.

This creates a problem for a left whose vision of a revolutionary politic happens largely outside the state because it cannot rely on the same opportunism that the right has. For example, the religious right and organizations like the Federalist Society played a long game through decades of education and training to instill their values into key institutions that would then reshape civil society. We aren't doing the same, because we envision the community in a different way. But what is our long game to build up a radical, antifascist, and leftist political consciousness? This is the question that demands an answer more than anything else, and it likely lies in the growth of labor and tenant unions, mutual aid networks, and other community projects that reach directly into the areas most abandoned by social services and strengthen their resilience apart from the state. There are options to engage some version of the state apparatus, from plans, inspired by the writings of political philosopher Murray Bookchin, to hold neighborhood assemblies tied to regional elected positions (such as neighborhood councils or associations), to efforts to influence state institutions through coordinated social movements. But our power must remain in the community, not tied to tax dollars, restrictive codes of conduct, and the limitations of an electoral system designed to disempower average people. Instead, we have to grow in all areas of social life; only then can we eradicate the fertilizer that allows fascist movements to bloom.

This is why we have to see the threat fascism poses to movements for justice for liberation as coming from two directions, the inside and the outside, both of which seek to completely eradicate our efforts to build a radically different world. Across world history, fascist movements have targeted what the society in which they emerge sees as a particularly villainized minority, but also the movements that try to build power for those victimized by the ruling classes. When Italy's National Fascist Party took power, they immediately crushed the labor movement, understanding that a union is a way for working-class people who are disenfranchised to take power for themselves. Nazi Germany turned its sights first and foremost on the socialists and communists (a move deeply intertwined with their antisemitism), dreamy radicals who envisioned that the eradication of class and hierarchies themselves were what would cure the German working class. Inside of Israel, as the far right more fully takes power, the left has become nearly as demonized as Palestinians, portrayed as a betrayer-class. This is why when fascist movements like Lehava—formed to stop intermarriage between Jews and non-Jews—head into the streets, they attack perceived leftists with just as much frenzy as anyone else in their sites.

This is why antifascism, the movement that constitutes itself purely for the destruction of fascism, is not just an important part of coalitions for change; it is a necessity. That defensive mechanism is crucial for social movements to build to the scale necessary to challenge capital and build dual power, as well as to maintain the integrity of vision to win a new kind of world. Fascism is a real threat, one of the most pressing as the political center collapses and crisis becomes endemic as economic, ecological, and social stability falter. What activists building power in our communities must consider is what to do about this, how to protect themselves, and what it means to make antifascism an integral part of their world building. The way this looks is broad: mutual aid networks, labor unions, tenant organizing, all of which bore in on particular issues while connecting with the larger system—and all of which are a threat to power, and therefore vulnerable to the attacks that are coming. And this brings us immediately back to the first intervention: that community organizing to meet human need will ultimately be what neutralizes the regrowth of a fascist insurgency. But we have to be able to build for long enough to sustain it, and in an era of massive far-right threats, that means operating with the full knowledge that there are many who would rather make us victims than let us succeed.

If we want to consider the immediate threat of fascism, then those engaged in radical organizing of some type should consider three things so as to intervene.

The first, as discussed above, is that we often are recruiting from the same pool of potential participants—and that doesn't just mean in the depoliticized space. It's obvious that rural areas, for example, have been ripe for militia organizing, and that's often because that is the only radical political movement interfacing with those areas and offering dramatic "solutions" to real problems. But this potential shift to the far right can happen in areas we already consider in the process of radicalization, which are already joining a project we envision as essential to human liberation. As we head into an absolute calamity generated by climate change, deforestation, mass water pollution, and the destruction of wildland, the radical environmental movement is one of the most important projects we have today. In fact, environmentalism, particularly that evolving from the early-twentieth century as "conservationism," was in large part a right-wing movement. It questioned the established conventions of "civilization" and technology, and demanded an almost social Darwinist vision of "natural law"; for its adherents, the preservation of species was often tied directly to the idea of white survival as a supposed global racial minority. The environmental movement eventually moved toward the left, but after years in the wilderness taking positions against immigration, fearmongering about overpopulation, and casting blame for environmental destruction—often on those who do not fit in "traditionalist" models of community building. But even as the green movement became set firmly in the realm of the left, far-right ideas continued to seep in, whether by the return of a kind of enviro-pessimism under the guise of deep ecology and biocentrism, or via transphobic authoritarian cadres like "anti-civilization" group Deep Green Resistance, which has called for a type of guerilla war against the instruments of industrial civilization.

When I was in Earth First! years back, relatively recent memories of anti-immigrant beliefs that permeated some groups, including talk of eugenics, open sexism, and scaremongering about "overpopulation." This history should not taint the modern incarnations of Earth First!, but we know what kinds of reactionary impulses remain possible in this space, and we have to be aware of where these ideas can drift.

This problem is only going to escalate as ecofascism becomes one of the primary ways that the right, and even those who consider themselves beyond the political binary, engage with the increasingly volatile questions of dwindling resources. "What we're seeing is a turn on the right away from denial of climate change, and toward an ecofascist position," Reece Jones, a scholar of anti-immigrant movements, explained to me. "[The] notion that we have to protect our borders in order to protect our environment."[3] This was the foundation of the Tanton Network, a series of organizations created by white nationalist John Tanton—including the Federation for American Immigration Reform and Numbers USA—that now dominate discourse on immigration and have major influence in the Republican Party.[4] Previously involved in the Sierra Club, Tanton often tied his anti-immigrant xenophobia directly back to the protectionist perspective on the environment, a way of extending the panic many experience over

---

3. Reece Jones, quoted in Shane Burley, "White Borders Author Q&A with Reece Jones," *Political Research Associates*, April 28, 2022, https://politicalresearch.org/2022/04/28/white-borders.
4. Stan Cox, "Green Rationales for Harsher Immigration Policies Are Nothing New," *The Nation*, May 1, 2023, https://www.thenation.com/article/environment/ecofascism-immigration-fair.

the destruction of the earth to the racist impulsivity we have seen with regard to immigrants moving over the southern US border. This became even more obvious during the Trump years as mass shooters, such as the assailant in the 2019 El Paso murder spree, referenced fascist ideas openly.[5] We will continue to see workers pulled toward the far right through a concern over environmental catastrophe. The reason for this is simple: they are looking for radical solutions to a radical problem. We live in a bizarre time where most of what is erroneously called the "left" is asleep at the wheel, debating over carbon credits and recyclable plastics while the world heats past the point of salvation. This is a product of the profound limitation that our political imagination has experienced, where tepid liberalism is erroneously described as the "left," leaving the actual political left to exist mostly outside of the electoral realm. So, as what is generally portrayed as the mainstream green movement displays their own ineptitude to a growing audience of concerned activists, many of them are going to assume this means the left has little to offer in the way of preventing ecological suicide. Instead of finding revolutionary voices, like those we want to mobilize, these seekers can also find those offering a different pathway, one that validates their internal biases while offering them a cookie-cutter form of radicalism.

The green movement is not unique; this is true across almost every type of social movement, which has seen right-wing entryism and, just as common, people bringing fascist ideas into organizing spaces out of a certain naive genuineness. The anti-war movement, the labor movement, international solidarity, and just about every other coalition fighting for justice has experienced a version of this, and we often ignore this problem out of the need to generate the numbers necessary for a mass movement.

---

5. Alexandra Minna Stern, "White Nationalists' Extreme Solution to the Coming Environmental Apocalypse," *The Conversation*, August 22, 2019, https://theconversation.com/white-nationalists-extreme-solution-to-the-coming-environmental-apocalypse-121532.

But this dissonance creates a fatal crack in our design, and allowing those ideas uncritical access to our movements creates an infection that can quickly become incurable. The way around this is, however, something we already understand quite well: we have to agitate, educate, and organize. The way to create a viable strategy is to hold a relatively clear picture of what is causing our problems, and the way to build consensus is to ensure that those entering a movement have a clear educational pathway to learn more so they can participate in an egalitarian environment. Clarity of vision and capacity to train are the fastest ways to establish standards and boundaries for what a particular movement is going to be. Intersectionality is another piece, showing people how crises do not exist in isolation but are part of a larger system of racial capitalism and settler colonialism. By doing that, we undermine the notion that, for example, environmental degradation is caused by "mass immigration" or "feminine consumerism" and craft in its place a recognizable picture for people demanding answers. Most people pulled into conspiracy theories or far-right social movements engage with them because they are searching and so helping them on the path to answers is not just individually healthy; it is an act of self-defense. This should not mean that we create a uniform ideological culture where debate is stifled and a diversity of opinions is disallowed but, instead, that we discover a baseline agreement where people can know, intimately, what they are a part of.

It's also important to note that the far right's perception of who they can recruit has expanded dramatically in recent decades. There are an accelerating number of fascist groups, even white nationalist projects, that invite members of color, just as there are openly nationalist queer-led organizations and anti-feminist cadres run by women. Whatever community we think should be naturally drawn to our politics, there is an opponent who believes they should have access to them as well.

The second piece of this puzzle is establishing community self-defense as a necessary part of all organizing. As discussed above, a certain frame of interrelationality drives this work when we are adapting antifascism to the needs of other social movements. If we are police and prison abolitionists, then we must find a way to protect ourselves and solve problems outside of the carceral state. Antifascism is a way of defending those who are marginalized without going to the police, in the same way that transformative justice is a method of adjudicating internal harm without involving the state.

The primary reason for doing this is that all of the left, or even just organized efforts by marginalized communities to improve daily life, are under vicious assault from the right. When the second eruption of Black Lives Matter exploded into the streets in 2020, there were around a hundred car attacks, mostly from far-right ideologues, and many street beatings, gang jumpings, and knife and baton strikes against organizers.[6] The same kind of violence marked 2022 and 2023's Pride season as far-right "anti-groomer" groups and white nationalists like the Patriot Front went after queer events, issuing threats against drag shows and even trans health care facilities, libraries, and youth organizations.[7] Any project worth building will be seen as a threat by the far-right, and if we achieve the scale necessary to really win something, then reactionaries will likely see us as a problem to be destroyed.

There is a reason that "antifa" has become the boogeyman for the entire right, the central ghoul for the newest incarnation of

---

6. Lex LcMenamin, "How Cars Became a Deadly Anti-Protest Weapon," *Mic*, December 30, 2020, https://www.mic.com/impact/how-cars-became-a-deadly-anti-protest-weapon-53291831; Shane Burley and Alexander Reid Ross, "Conspiracy Theories by Cops Fuel Far Right Attacks against Antiracist Protesters," *Truthout*, September 18, 2020, https://www.truthout.org/articles/conspiracy-theories-by-cops-fuel-far-right-attacks-against-antiracist-protesters.

7. Change Che, "5 White Nationalist Group Members Convicted in Plans to Riot at Pride Event," *New York Times*, July 21, 2023, https://www.nytimes.com/2023/07/21/us/patriot-front-idaho-pride-convicted.html.

classic anti-communist conspiracy theories.[8] Antifascists create an implicit dysfunction in the right by disrupting their proceedings, protecting those radicals who fascists deem enemies, and making the right's ideology and behavior public knowledge. The centrality of antifa to the far-right mythos has been largely constructed out of whole cloth, but there is a working logic to their decision to do so: they need to eradicate the defensive mechanism if they are to fully destroy their enemies. More than this, as the larger right further radicalizes, it wants to do so while claiming its opponents are the ones breaking democratic norms. That can only happen if the movement to confront their accelerating violence is in shambles and cannot interfere in their business of building the future.

Antifascism Should Be Everywhere

The world of radical organizing is just as subject to trend cycles as the rest of modern society. In a 2024 presentation from a longtime antifascist organizer, I listened as he lamented the fact that in Portland, Oregon, often thought of as a heart of militant antifascism, so few of the established organizations were in the room. The reason was obvious: those organizations had largely collapsed. Many swelled, or were birthed, at the end of the 2010s as the encroachment of fascism had a sense of urgency attached to it. But time moves on, other movements take our attention, and Trumpism, the alt-right, and the American far right became institutionalized and old news. The world of radical politics has changed, where long-standing organizations take on less importance and flexible and horizontal social networks become the norm. Many of these networks center around particular issues, some mix of ad hoc confederations, existing projects, and even just individuals, rapidly building something that looks like a social

---

8. Shane Burley, *Why We Fight: Essays on Fascism, Resistance, and Surviving the Apocalypse* (Chico: AK Press, 2021).

movement. For millennials and Gen Z, this has been the reality for most of our lives: the anti-war movement in early 2000s, Occupy Wall Street, Black Lives Matter, antifascist mobilizations, and, starting in 2023, the movement to stop the genocide in Gaza. And while this new movement infrastructure demands fluidity and adaptability, we need to locate consistency as well. What makes these movements so dynamic is that people come in with existing skills, relationships, and even organizations, but that they allow those resources to flex according to the new conditions.

What this means is that it is useful to build up particular specializations and assemblances of people while acknowledging that the work may change at a moment's notice. As antifascism became the cause de jure across the US with the rise of the alt-right and Trump, many people left other projects to join antifascist groups or start new ones, and when the public profile of antifascism waned, many of those groups subsequently collapsed. What the social movement landscape demands is long-term commitment to a particular type of work, and choosing an individual project or lane to invest in does not mean a lack of commitment to all the others. Instead, we should focus not just on how to get people involved in antifascist organizing but how to make antifascist organizing a service for other types of social movements and mass actions. The labor movement is in a period of left-turn growth. How can antifascists protect picket lines and defend against far-right infiltration? Mutual aid may be the essential organizing piece for the twenty-first century, but given that many of the community who are looking for partnership and support (such as sex workers or those living in houseless encampments) are also a direct target of fascist hooligans, how can mutual aid groups partner with antifascists to keep everyone safe and neighborhoods clear? What we want to cultivate is not singular organizations but instead numerous groups and projects all working in some degree of coordination and collaboration.

For those thinking about antifascism and where it fits, the first question to answer is, what groups and movements already exist? Are they sufficient to keep other projects safe? What could make them reach the capacity we need? If something is missing, who could create a group, and what would it take to give it life? And, most importantly, how can we plug that antifascist consortium into the larger network of social movements? Is there a larger network?

What makes antifascism work is largely what makes any type of mass movement work, and its only future is one where cross-organizational and movement collaboration is the norm. Organizations will rise and fall more rapidly than before, while others remain temporary or barely visible, but these coalitions are often a proxy for building up human relationships, shared ideas, and infrastructures that are not simply owned by a particular organization. When we collaborate, those are human beings working together, building relationships that can outlast the projects that started them and injecting skills into the community that participates. Social media tools have allowed incredibly sophisticated methodologies to be built and rebuilt with exponentially quickening speed, and if we make coalitions our starting point, then we will ensure that even when some groups go the way of the dinosaur, the relationships and growth they achieved will be injected back into the communities.

Ultimately, what stops fascism's ascendance is not an antifascist movement but a viable plan to target the amelioration that pulls people into reactionary politics in the first place, such as economic instability or the lack of close familial and communal ties. As rural communities are economically devastated and stripped of social services, as the Rust Belt continues to be hollowed out by diminishing jobs and falling real wages, and where very real dislocation is recast as the consequence of progressive social changes, a segment of the working class is being primed for a radicalism not of our own design. If we are not in those communities, building relationships and tackling the issues that matter to them, if we write them off or distance ourselves from their struggles, then no amount of defensive maneuvering will stop the right from entirely capturing the fire that capitalism's contradictions have ignited.

Antifascism is not a fixed position; it is a mobile framework to create a casing that can protect whatever the insurgency is that is desperately trying to challenge power. And because assault and infiltration are to be expected, defense is integral. So, what every organizer needs to consider is not just how antifascism can become a vibrant movement in its own right, but how to bring it into the wider social movement patchwork we are going to have to sew if we want to see the kind of revolutionary tipping points we so often demand. Without that, our failure is guaranteed.

Yours in struggle,
Shane

Shane Burley is a journalist and filmmaker based in Portland, Oregon. He is the author and editor of four books, including *¡No Pasaran!: Antifascist Dispatches from a World in Crisis* (AK Press and the Institute for Anarchist Studies, 2022) and *Safety Through Solidarity: A Radical Guide to Fighting Antisemitism* (coauthored with Ben Lorber; Melville House, 2024). His work has been featured in places like *NBC News, The Daily Beast, Jacobin, Al Jazeera, Truthout, In These Times, Jewish Currents, The Baffler, Yes! Magazine,* and *Oregon Humanities.*

Read This if You Are Overwhelmed by Attacks on Reproductive Autonomy

Renee Bracey Sherman

Dear Organizer,

    I must be honest. At the moment I am writing this, I am feeling a lot of despair, frustration, and anger. Right now, when I look around at the status of the reproductive health, rights, and justice movements, I feel let down. *Roe* fell. The moment we all knew would happen—the moment we went hoarse in our throats warning about—happened. We had to beg the president of the United States to even *say* the word "abortion." Clinics are shuttering, and people are being arrested for having abortions and miscarriages. Politicians and advocates are calling for reproductive freedom as we send countless bombs to the homes of mamas and babies in Palestine and beyond. For those of us seeking reproductive healthcare, we've seen how reproductive freedom was only a reality for those who could afford it, yet the pain of seeing the gatekeeping by our friends and foes alike never stops hurting. And, the reality is that I know it's going to get worse before it gets better.

    Despite the popularity of abortion and clear electoral wins since the fall of *Roe*, actual access to abortion care isn't reachable for most. We are on a hamster wheel of election cycles with new promises stacked on the previously broken ones. Ideas to rebuild our country are littered with solutions that end in hyper-surveillance and carcerality rather than investment in our loved ones and communities. Our political allies are not willing to see how their tough-on-crime policies and unending investment in wars and policing hurt our calls for abortion liberation. Their visions are short sighted: the more they invest in police, the more they invest in the very apparatus that investigates and arrests people for having abortions and miscarriages while surveilling those who take the risks of bringing abortion pills into this country and distributing them in our communities. Their appeasement of the war machine is destroying abortion access and the brittle system we're trying to keep afloat for their loved ones.

Everyone loves someone who had an abortion. We need to fucking act like it.

I don't think I'm asking for a lot. My vision for the future is simple: I want a world in which everyone has the love and resources to decide what to do with their pregnancies. I want a world in which everyone can have free abortions, whenever they want. I want a world in which everyone can decide if, when, and how to grow their families and have the time to spend with their loved ones without worry. I want abortion to be liberated. I want all of that for everyone and nothing less.

As simple as my vision is, I know it is a world I may never experience. There are days I feel despondent at best. Most days, simmering coals of anger sit in my chest like heartburn. It's not healthy. I feel disappointed. A lot. Being a leftist can be demoralizing. I see us working against ourselves by failing to offer our comrades the very basic things we advocate for in our messaging: living wages, paid parental leave, accessible abortions, the promise of reproductive justice. We make it unaffordable for people in our own movement to create the families they want and to spend time with their loved ones. We deserve to experience the beauty of the world we're advocating for.

Sometimes I show up to meetings antagonistic and nihilistic about the future. I am tired. I am burning out. Yet, I still have to get up every day and try to lead a community of people who've had abortions toward reproductive justice. There is so much to do, from the mundane paperwork to the heartwarming moments. Picking up abortion patients at the airport and driving them to their appointments is a welcomed break from conference calls and budget reviews. Retreats and conferences with abortion storytellers from my organization fills my soul because it's a reminder that we will keep on speaking out, no matter the cost. As the frustration seeps in when there's another abortion ban or a politician says something harmful or undermining of people of color who need an abortion, I feel renewed when I can brainstorm a campaign with our team that will joyfully counter the narratives and stereotypes of people who have abortions.

It's a swing of emotions that I have become used to and try to harden against. I have burned out before, and sometimes I think I am on the brink of it again. The uncertainty makes it hard for me to be sure of what I am feeling at any given moment. Sometimes I can feel the disassociation taking over—I think that's normal. We're in the middle of a genocide and a hostile fascist takeover of our nation. And, abortion was one of the first issues they attacked hard. We've been sustaining devastating losses for over a decade. We're experiencing collective grief, and we've never taken a pause to process all that has happened. It's a lot for us abortion organizers to recover from—especially those of us of color and who've had abortions. Sometimes, I am overtaken by the survivor's guilt of being able to have an abortion when so many cannot.

Yet, we continue on. We try for another ballot initiative. We open another clinic. We drive another patient to their appointment. We launch another campaign. We distribute abortion pills in our community. We protest. We answer the abortion-fund hotlines. We share our abortion stories. We testify. We survive.

One thing I know for sure is that when I take myself out of the humdrum of life, I can reset and reconnect with myself and my vision for abortion liberation. It's easy to get lost in your purpose when paperwork and politics take precedent. What I do know is that we have all that we need right now to rebuild abortion access. Our communities, against all odds, are holding strong. We can't lose sight of the vision for reproductive justice that we imagine. When it feels like we're losing it all, we have to remember that we have the people on our side. When we go outside and organize our neighbors and loved ones, that is what will restore our faith in justice and build the reproductive future we desire and deserve.

It's easier said than done, of course. But I've never regretted a day I spent talking with people about that vision or ensuring someone can share their abortion story or gets their abortion as easily as possible.

I don't have the answers for you, but my advice is a reminder to *live* in this world, and in this moment, with joy. It will fuel you as an activist, and the human being you are first and foremost. The best I can offer you is a meditation on things I did this year to reconnect with myself, my body, and my hopes for the future. In trying to think of how to tell you how to approach these times, it came out like this.

Never be so busy that you can't stop and smell the sweet roses of a neighbor's garden or blossoms of a magnolia tree. Lay on the earth and read a book until you have no idea what time it is. Feel each blade of grass between your toes. Let your nipples float free in the ocean. Drench yourself in the warmth of the sun. Build with people who hold your same liberatory and leftist values so you know you're not alone. That connection has grown me as an activist and as a human. Dance until you've sweated it all out. Eat meals that you think about years later. Play with your food. Play with children. Sit with their vision of what the world can be. Sleep in. Touch yourself in the way only you know you like. Fuck. Get fucked. Allow yourself to experience everything we want for others and more. Then, come back to your vision of what you want the world to be, while loving the beauty that is already in it. And remind others to do the same. It's how we'll build toward reproductive justice. It's how I am making my vision a reality.

Sincerely,
Renee

Renee Bracey Sherman is an abortion activist, writer, and founder of We Testify, an organization dedicated to the leadership and representation of people who have abortions. She is also the coauthor of *Liberating Abortion: Claiming Our History, Sharing Our Stories, and Building the Reproductive Future We Deserve* (Amistad, 2024) and cohost of the podcast *The A Files: A Secret History of Abortion*, both in collaboration with Regina Mahone.

Read This if Injustice Has Alienated You from Your Community

Maya Schenwar

Dear Anti-Zionist Jewish Organizer,

 I'm writing to you in March of 2024, in the midst of Israel's intensified genocide against the people of Gaza. Israel, backed by the US, has killed thirty-one thousand people, injured so many more, and is starving and displacing untold numbers while flattening the landscape of their home.

 Israel is slaughtering people as they wait in line for food, even as—like the UN and World Food Program have repeated—everyone in Gaza is hungry.

 Israel is systematically driving people out of their towns only to bomb the areas to which they've fled. People are without water or shelter, dying of infectious disease, dying buried under the rubble, often dying uncounted.

 Israel is deliberately shattering whole families and communities, then demolishing the infrastructure upon which they might build again, trying to ensure they never build again, trying to create conditions in which they will not live to build.

 It is a holocaust.

 By the time you read this, is it being recognized as such? I don't know whether it will be months, years, decades, or centuries, but, as Palestinian novelist and activist Susan Abulhawa writes in *Electronic Intifada*, eventually history "will record that Israel perpetrated a holocaust in the 21st century."

Opposition to this holocaust is—flabbergastingly—not currently a popular stance in many Jewish quarters. Within those quarters, dissent is being smothered.

All around me, anti-Zionist Jewish friends are being forced out of their employment at "progressive" Zionist Jewish institutions. Most of the part-time employees of the anti-Zionist congregation I attend in Chicago have resigned or been fired from their day jobs at mainstream liberal Jewish institutions that refuse to acknowledge the genocide. Beyond job loss, many of my anti-Zionist Jewish friends have had their immediate family, coworkers, and lifelong friends cut ties. I bet you're also witnessing this. Words I hear again and again from my community: "lonely," "rejected," "alienated," even "disowned."

For me, the past few months' severings have been minor by comparison, but still, some friends, acquaintances, former coworkers, former classmates, and countless strangers on the internet have denounced my writings, the actions I've co-organized, and my other public displays of anti-Zionism—on social media, in comments online, in emails and messages, and through simply disappearing from my life.

Sometimes I get lost in thought loops, wondering how it is remotely possible that people, some of whom I used to think of as "my people"—many of whom claim to be aligned with progressivism, human rights, and even anti-colonial and anti-imperial sensibilities, and whose ancestors died in pogroms and the Nazi holocaust—are cutting off relationships in service of defending a fascist power.

Are you getting lost in these thought loops, too? And are you also angry at yourself (Jewish-guilty?) for wasting time obsessing about this bullshit?

The loops sometimes keep me up at night, but ultimately, they really are circular: no end point, and maybe, no point whatsoever.

Transformation Means Something

In November, I joined more than a hundred others in blockading the entrance to Chicago's Israeli consulate. As we shut down Ogilvie Train Station, we were mass-arrested. When I got out, some videos I'd posted to Instagram had (unusually) gone viral and were being met with a torrent of jeers from trolls, and even from some people I knew. Some trolls (and a couple of former friends) seized on images of my arrest on social media, asking how I would like to be held hostage by Hamas. Someone asked: "Why didn't they throw away the key?"

This shouldn't have hit me like a gut punch; after all, in my work as a writer and editor, I've experienced twenty years of haters and trolls. And these people asking me whether I'd like to be held hostage were not my people, right? Why did I care what they thought?

But obviously, the question of "my people" is fraught—particularly for the many of us who grew up viewing ourselves as part of a broad community from which we're now profoundly alienated.

As a young child, I lived in Chicago's West Rogers Park neighborhood, in a predominantly Jewish enclave. Each day after kindergarten, I would walk two blocks to my mom's children's bookstore (yes, these were different times!), which sat on the same block as the Jewish Community Center (JCC), the Jewish deli, the Jewish bakery, and so on. I knew I could get a cookie from the bakery just by walking in and smiling. I knew at the deli, they'd fork over a sample (a whole slice!) of muenster cheese. At the JCC, my grandpa would be playing pinochle, eating a kosher hot dog, and talking about how the kosher hot dog only cost seventy-five cents. Once, I got lost, and an Orthodox mom with nine kids helped deposit me back at my mom's store. I felt held by this community.

Nowadays, an Israeli flag hangs in the window of that kosher bakery; of course, I won't go inside. I stop at a grocery store in the neighborhood on the way back from a protest and notice people averting their eyes from me in my "Not in My Name" shirt. I remember that many probably see me as the "enemy" in what was once my home.

I'm hit with angry disappointment when my childhood synagogue—where my own fire for social justice was kindled amid the radical Sanctuary Movement, which supported undocumented migrants against cruel government forces—releases a flimsy statement on the "crisis in Israel-Palestine." The statement avoids the word "genocide," framing this ongoing massacre as a complicated both-sides conflict. It calls for "peace" and says nothing.

I shouldn't care what liberal genocide deniers are doing or saying. It's not the point. The thought loops again!

Are you feeling this tension, arguing with ghosts?

For many anti-Zionist Jewish organizers, a sense of deep alienation pervades our efforts, not only because we have been cut off from current mainstream Jewish institutions but because we're experiencing breaks with communities that shaped our earlier senses of self, in some cases at least partly defining our senses of self.

This type of alienation isn't singularly Jewish—far from it! Most organizers, most *people*, experience it in one way or another, this severing from the way you thought things were. It's worth acknowledging it—not dwelling in it, given that we're in the midst of fighting a genocide—but acknowledging that it's there and real nonetheless.

It is also worth acknowledging that in comparison to those communities and narratives we've lost, we are, well, *right*. Many of our Jewish communities of origin tell us that we misunderstand, that we're eschewing complexity, that we don't have the *real* information. But chances are—unless you were raised anti-Zionist or outside of Zionism, or came to Judaism later in life—you have navigated a circuitous and difficult path of transformation to get to this place, sorting through lifelong webs of propaganda and deep wells of emotional betrayal; learning from Palestinian organizers and friends, from books and media, from your co-strugglers' stories.

I hope you can take a minute to set aside your Jewish guilt (let's not prove those Zionists right about us being "self-hating"!) and recognize your own transformation, because it reminds you, us, that humans can transform—a central principle to hold close in all our work as organizers. This recognition of your own progress doesn't have to be self-congratulatory or ostentatious. It can be humble (after all, you used to be *wrong*!), and can be meaningful and necessary to sustaining your work for the long haul.

Growing up, my parents were taught to send "tzedakah" to plant trees in Israel—a seemingly beneficent gesture that, in reality, is part of the Zionist project of annihilating Palestinian villages. They took me on Chicago's Walk With Israel when I was a child. But later, they, too, went through a reckoning. Now, my parents belong to Tzedek, the first anti-Zionist congregation in the US, to which I belong; they have a "Stop the Genocide" sticker on their front door in the colors of the Palestinian flag; they attend ceasefire protests; they push back against Zionist rhetoric in their own long-standing circles and are always learning. That means something.

In these kinds of transformations, I see power, I find hope.

Where do you find hope? What transformations have you witnessed—transformations that have stuck? Maybe this is one way we can move beyond our thought loops.

Who Are Our People? What Are We Doing?

This morning, my five-year-old kid and I walked a few blocks through East Rogers Park to where Tzedek holds its family program every other Sunday. We sang in Hebrew, Arabic, and English, and we made art for a free Palestine, which we taped along the street.

I caught the eyes of other parents as we watched our kids scribble "Ceasefire Now" and "Free Palestine" in red, green, and black crayon.

This morning at the family program, I didn't eat the challah—a fast I've been practicing these last months. I'm part of organizing an effort called Jewish Fast for Gaza, cofounded by rabbis Brant Rosen (my rabbi, and an outspoken anti-Zionist) and Brian Walt. In the Jewish tradition of fasting as an act of mourning and a call to action, we have been fasting weekly for the past twenty-one weeks. We've committed to continue fasting weekly until a ceasefire. Each week, we experience a small sliver of hunger—nothing compared to what people in Gaza are put through daily—and it serves as a visceral reminder that we need to disrupt, to interrupt, to refuse to surrender to the normal flow of life while a genocide rages. Each week as we fast, we recommit to action, following and joining our Palestinian co-strugglers.

Last night, Jewish Fast for Gaza co-organized a night of local Palestinian and MENA art, music and poetry, along with other groups in our community: Students for Justice in Palestine, Loyola; the P.O. Box Collective; and Rad Rogers Park. The artists shared their paths toward creating and imagining during this heartbreaking and enraging time. The musicians sang in Arabic, songs of hope for a day of return and freedom. The community that gathered included people who've been taking action, over and over, to push for an end to Israel's rampage and, ultimately, to settler-colonialism.

During these two hours, I let go of the thought loops about "my people" and their genocide denial. Instead, I looked around the room and thought: *These* are my people. People who reject colonization, who will do nearly anything to stop a genocide. People who are drawing from their own experiences and lineages—of diaspora, of Indigeneity, of spiritual teachings, of questioning and of truth. People who know that solidarity is the only way forward.

Mainstream Jewish institutions—even though they share one of my adjectives, "Jewish"—are not mine. They're not yours. And if we can't convince them (and I'm feeling, at this particular moment, that maybe we just can't), we have to release them and find our real people.

This complete break with mainstream Jewish institutions may fire up our sense of alienation. It may sometimes prompt us to ask: Who the fuck are we?

Does it matter?

Maybe it doesn't matter at all, in the grand scheme. (I recall a recent discussion in which another anti-Zionist Jew groaned, "We have to stop talking about saving the Jewish soul!") But for me, Jewishness can be a motivator for sustained action (and so, oddly, the opposite of guilt). For me, it means drawing from some of the traditions of my ancestors—those that actually make sense to me—and relinquishing the ones that don't. Those sustaining traditions include recognizing our historical memory as people on the move, making community wherever we've ended up in diaspora; surviving through solidarities; questioning and challenging authority; starting revolutions; and honoring *pikuach nefesh*, the idea that saving a life is what must guide us above all else. We are living in these lineages even as we co-create something new.

In sifting through my grandfather's things after he died a few years ago, I found a folder of my great-grandfather's pamphlets and flyers and writings. He was a communist, a radical, and an immigrant who fled Eastern Europe amid rampant antisemitism. These three overlapping identities characterize many of my ancestors—a not-uncommon combination.

In my great-grandfather's folder, I found pamphlets, more than a half century old, denouncing Zionism and citing Zionism's antisemitic origins. Anti-Zionism (including Jewish anti-Zionism) is as old as Zionism. And it is strengthening by the day because more and more people are actively practicing it.

In moments when you're thinking, "Who the fuck am I?" sometimes it's helpful to counter that with, "What the fuck am I doing?" In *Let This Radicalize You* (coauthored by Kelly Hayes and Mariame Kaba), Mariame writes in her introduction, "The most important thing you can do to transform the world is to act." Along these lines, Palestinian journalist Mohammed el-Kurd recently wrote in a *Mondoweiss* essay, "It is tempting, almost comforting—particularly as I look at the food on my table and the roof over my head—to indulge in guilt, but it is an unproductive sentiment, it does not start revolutions."

Another reason to set aside our Jewish guilt: We need that energy for revolution, right?

Water and Love and Solidarity

Steven Salaita's beautiful book *An Honest Living* came out recently. Have you read it? I appreciated his deep meditation on alienation. He was shut out of academia for years after being fired from a tenured position due to his criticism of Israel, and a lot of the book follows his path of finding meaning and connection outside of prestigious "white collar" work. As I write to you now about alienation and connection, I think of a line from the book in which Salaita is talking about the culture of metropolitan Washington, DC, residential neighborhoods: "Amid a landscape of spies, lobbyists, consultants, and politicians, alien life exists in ribbons of unrefined habitation. Here, notions of community govern the social contract. . . . Hell, sometimes children even spontaneously knock on doors and ask their friends to come outside."

My hope for us is not that we can convince the mainstream Jewish community to get on our page, or that I can be welcomed into the halls of the West Rogers Park Jewish Community Center in my "Not in Our Name" shirt. Rather, my hope for us is to exist in "ribbons of unrefined habitation." That sounds like connective potential to me. I want to knock on my friends' doors! It sounds like love.

Melanie Kaye/Kantrowitz, the late founder of Jews for Racial and Economic Justice, countered the Zionist specter of a genocidal ethnostate with her vision of radical diasporism: "Diasporism cherishes love across the borders. . . . Our vehicle is not the bloodline but culture, history, memory. Diasporists recognize our identity as simultaneously rock, forged under centuries of pressure, and water, infinitely flexible."

So maybe that's who the fuck we are: rock and water, both surviving and flexible—surviving through our flexibility. And in our flexibility, we connect. We try to build new solidarities across borders of all the kinds.

In an essay about being fired from their job at a liberal Zionist congregation, my friend Adam Gottlieb emphasizes the importance of remembering the long Jewish tradition of creative community building: "Our central story of liberation, our millennia of experience surviving in the diaspora through solidarity with others... all remind us that our very existence continually moves us to seek liberation from narrow places, like water flowing, as it freely does, from the river to the sea."

So, water. Water travels across borders, and as Kaye/Kantrowitz reminds us, so does love.

Another great book came out last year, which takes a Kaye/Kantrowitz line as its title: *Solidarity Is the Political Version of Love*. The book is by Rebecca Vilkomerson and Rabbi Alissa Wise, movement leaders of Jewish Voice for Peace. "Whatever your version of solidarity, may you practice it as an expression of love," they write. "A love that manifests as raging at the world as it is, and at the same time developing smart, intentional plans to realize the world as it should be.... Love, like solidarity, lives in the both/and."

Friend! I hope you are holding close to your love and your solidarity, even in the moments when you feel most betrayed and rejected. I hope that in these moments, you can draw inspiration from diasporic ancestors and flowing water, and let yourself move, wandering toward where you're needed, where you can connect. And then connect, and then—as ever—act.

With love and in solidarity,
Maya

Maya Schenwar is director of the Truthout Center for Grassroots Journalism and the board president and editor-at-large at *Truthout*. She is the coeditor, with Kim Wilson, of *We Grow the World Together: Parenting Toward Abolition* (Haymarket Books, 2024) and coauthor, with Victoria Law, of *Prison by Any Other Name: The Harmful Consequences of Popular Reforms* (The New Press, 2021). Maya is cofounder of Media Against Apartheid and Displacement, a journalism hub uplifting Palestine-focused reporting, and she organizes with Love & Protect and Jewish Fast for Gaza.

Read This if You Are a Discouraged Incarcerated Organizer

Stevie Wilson

Dear Comrade,

    Organizing is full of setbacks and repression, especially if you are an imprisoned organizer. You may experience solitary confinement, transfers, and destruction of property. These repressive acts may leave you reeling with strong emotions: anger, frustration, fear, and despair. I know these emotions well. I have been transferred to four prisons in four years. And the guards trashed all of my books and paperwork. Encountering repression proves one thing: you are doing something right. You are becoming a menace to our enemies. Thank you.

    Their behavior is typical tyrant conduct. Prison officials know that organizing imprisoned people creates collective power that can be used to change conditions of confinement and forge pathways to freedom. So they move quickly to squash efforts that build collectivity behind the walls. But, as Abdullah Ibrahim said: "They thought they could get rid of us by moving us to another place. But nothing in the universe goes away. It all returns." Comrade, you may have been transferred or placed in solitary confinement. It doesn't mean you have been defeated.

    As organizers, we are often called to transform injustices, to move through hardship toward a new possibility. But during periods of crisis, we are susceptible to forgetting what we are capable of and how we and others have made it through before. And you will make it through. I have. And I want to share some things that got me through solitary confinement, transfers, and the destruction of property. I want to share what enabled me to move through crisis and uncertainty, to see my condition through new eyes, and to continue to build collectivity behind the walls.

First, I took care of myself. And so should you. After my first transfer, I was filled with mixed emotions, and I needed to make space and time to process them. If I didn't, I wouldn't be any good to myself or others. Mariame Kaba and Kelly Hayes remind us to "take seriously the daily, personal practices that can nurture our well-being." For me, those practices have included journaling, exercising, and staying connected to friends. Take time to recommit to the practices that have and continue to help sustain you and the work.

This is a time when you should become a noticer, growing greater awareness of yourself, and what and who is around you. Doing so will enable you to listen for the relationship between *what is* and *what is possible*. Becoming a noticer will support your practice of being present. And being present will enable you to see opportunities where you can support your new community when the time is right.

Notice who people turn to for help. In order to survive behind these walls, we need each other. Wherever you are, there are people who other imprisoned people turn to for guidance and assistance. Whom do others ask for help and information? These people are organic leaders you will need to engage. Notice who is reading, and what they are reading. Whether in the yard or on the block, people are reading. These folx could be the first ones you distribute zines and books to. Notice what people are talking about, what concerns them most. These topics become springboards for you to introduce larger topics and connect struggles. They are also avenues for you to be of assistance to others, broadening and deepening their knowledge and understanding.

The prison aims to isolate, alienate, and disconnect us from each other and the world beyond the walls. Once they isolate and disconnect us, prison officials feel they can oppress us with impunity. Keeping us disconnected is key to their oppression. This is why they throw us into solitary confinement, transfer us away from friends, destroy our property, and withhold mail. Our connections counter and stymie their oppression. The stronger your connections, the more resilience and resistance you can generate. Consider your connections the batteries of your organizing and activism. They are also key to your survival behind the walls.

I keep a binder of notes and quotations on organizing and liberation, and in the process of writing this letter, I came back to one I wrote down by Harsha Walia: "We are only as strong as the constellation of communities that hold us up." Walia goes on to say: "What support can they offer publicly and privately to defuse the individual targeting?" Now is the time to lean upon and into those communities you belong to. Tap into your community connections. That is where your strength lies. That is where you will find possibility.

During and after each one of my transfers, after each act of repression, I depended upon my connections, my communities, to make it through. I needed people to make calls and advocate for my release from solitary confinement and for my safety. After my property was destroyed, my communities sent me more materials and funds. After one transfer, I discovered my typewriter was damaged beyond repair because it had been wrongly routed to another prison. My support network raised funds to purchase me a new typewriter, enabling me to continue my studies and work.

Your connections, your being in community, will make your transition into the new prison easier. Whether by calling the prison, organizing visits, or by sending you comforting letters, your connections can work against the feelings of alienation and loneliness you may feel upon entering a new place. As Maya Schenwar and Victoria Law write, "Creating community—connecting—is itself a political action in the face of systems meant to disconnect, confine, isolate and silence." Use and strengthen your connections right now to help you exercise self-care and re-establish your work.

Remember, as an organizer, you get one chance, and only one chance, to enter into a community. If the first impression people have of you is that you're arrogant, demeaning, or, even worse, a charlatan, you will never gain their trust and cooperation. A bad entry into a community can be an insurmountable barrier to gaining trust. And without trust, there is no organizing. Moving slowly, you will discover opportunities where you can assist the people, thereby earning their trust and respect. Moving slowly, you will be better able to discern what is happening and who is doing what. You will be able to identify potential collaborators. And you will need collaborators. There are limits to what any one individual can do to address problems that are structural and collective. You need a team.

You will also need time. Remember to keep things in perspective. The work of transformation is slow. Mariame Kaba writes: "To transform the conditions of our oppression(s), we can only do what we can do today, where we are, in the best way that we know." So do just that. Pace yourself. Gather your team. Because the work doesn't, and shouldn't, depend upon you alone. Kaba continues, "Uprooting oppression is the work of many lifetimes." We, imprisoned organizers, are paving the way for future fighters.

Whenever my cell was shaken down and my property damaged, whenever I was thrown in solitary confinement, whenever I was shackled and placed on a bus for transfer, whenever, after landing at a new prison, I discovered my property was missing, I would find myself asking: Why keep going? Why continue to fight? In the face of the prison's relentless oppression, giving up can seem like a smart choice—but it's not. The truth is that the work must be done. If it isn't, things—despite how bad they are now—will only get worse. Miski Noor and Kandace Montgomery, cofounders of the Black Visions Collective, have said: "We are in this work because our lives depend on it." And they do. Our lives and the lives of our communities, present and future, depend upon our work as imprisoned organizers.

As I said before, a crisis can cause one to forget what has been done and what is possible. This is why studying movement history is important. Our history guides and encourages us, especially during times of crisis. Whenever I face repression from the prison, I remember the contributions of political prisoner and Black anarchist Martin Sostre. I remember how he endured, how he kept up the fight against mail censorship, strip searches, the right to practice Islam, and won. We are still reaping the results of his struggles, struggles that happened in the 1960s and '70s. Martin was thrown in the hole. He was beaten. His property was trashed. He was transferred. He was forced to max out his sentence. And after release, he was framed and did nine more years before being commuted. All because he wanted freedom for the people! If he could endure all of that and keep going, so can I. And so can you.

Reading movement history will remind you that you are not alone. You are not the first to be harmed. And you won't be the last. You have a rich history to draw inspiration from. Spend time studying it. It will lift your head and heart. Read about the Angola Three. Learn how they kept going despite being framed and locked in solitary for decades. Read about Black communists organizing workers in 1930s Alabama during the height of Jim Crow and the Great Depression. Now, you know that if they could fight back during that time, we can do this work during our time. They faced death threats, violence, and discrimination every day. Read about Fred Cruz and David Ruiz, and their struggles in the Texas Department of Corrections. Read about George Jackson and Russell Maroon Shoatz. Reading movement history will provide you the sustenance you need to continue the fight, to build collective power behind the walls.

I hope these words have strengthened and deepened your commitment to organizing. I hope these words lift and strengthen your spirit. I hope they encourage you to continue to be a menace to our enemies. Because we need you. We need each other. Together is the only way we will win.

In solidarity,
Stevie

Stevie Wilson is a currently incarcerated Black and queer writer, activist, and student. He is a founding member of Dreaming Freedom, Practicing Abolition, a network of self-organized prisoner study groups building abolitionist community behind and across prison walls.

Read This if You Are Heartbroken

Ashon Crawley

To My Organizer Friends,

 We can make it. We can make it. But sometimes it does not feel this way.

 Have you ever been heartbroken? When I was in undergrad, I had a series of existential crises. I didn't realize it at the time, but it's true. I took a course titled Minorities and the Media—it was 2002, so the name of the course marks its historical moment in time. The course was about how racial, gender, and class representations in media matter, how they influence how we think about ourselves and the world. I was so convinced that I would do well in the class, that I already understood, that I took most of it with a grain of salt. We read about Black representations in film and I thought, Yes, this is all true. We read about Latinx representations, Asian and Asian American representations and women too.

 In each of these units, I was disturbed by the parallels, the ways each form of misrepresentation used politics and religion to denounce entire groups of people. Either the state was afraid of people taking resources—politics—or a spiritual community was concerned that people would adulterate all they considered holy—religion. I was curious how an entire group can become expendable and disposable, through leaps of logic and the imaginative failures that give people occasion to be unkind to others.

 It all made sense to me because it was within the domain of the familiar, even if the familiar was also disturbing. But the final unit was about queer representations in media—how gay and lesbian images in film, television, and journalism were deeply stereotypical and, also, how the disposability and caricaturing of gay and lesbian people used religious and political ideologies as the foundation. And this to say nothing of bisexual or trans or genderqueer practices of living. I noticed, as I had in the previous units, the consistencies, though I was also undone by them. Because if I accepted what we were learning in the classroom as true, I would have to reorient how I thought—and not just about textbooks and films and TV. If I were to be true to what I was learning, transformed by it, I would be forced to confront and reorient how I thought about myself, and the futures I could imagine differently.

And I was disoriented: what I was learning had the capacity to liberate me, but it felt suffocating, like I was slipping into quicksand. I knew I wanted to have integrity, so I could not comfortably and with conviction say, "But the Bible says being gay is sinful." The similarities were too noticeable. The professor was exacting in her pedagogy, and I wasn't even aware I was edging toward the gravitational field of truth beyond an event horizon of escape. But I also could not—because I was not ready to—say that I was wrong about the Bible regarding sexuality. So I stilled and quieted myself. I retreated from a lot of things in order to think and feel my way to another way of living. It was an existential crisis because I would need to change everything I thought I knew about myself, about others, about what God could be, about the world. I didn't have the will to fight for the doctrines of my religious upbringing. I no longer felt sure and certain. What could truth be in this situation when truth itself was being interrogated? I didn't know how to move forward. I was not necessarily stuck, but I was deeply ambivalent, a bit afraid too, because to think otherwise would mean giving up communities of care and concern that were formative, transformative, capacious, lush, and moving to me.

It took a long time, but I made it to the other side of the existential crisis. But it wasn't because I was smart or accomplished or read the right books. Reading, of course, helped, but that wasn't what held me in the difficulty. It was friendship. I had comrades that would think with me and lament with me and push me to ask more questions and would let me be heartbroken over and over again. And I still have them today. Because once the ruse of the world I *knew* to be correct and true and impervious to change shattered, I began to sense how it is precisely that imperviousness and need for certainty that needed to be relinquished; it is the very thing that makes so many of us unsafe to others, to the earth, to ourselves. The crisis of meaning I experienced about my queerness opened up a way for me to interrogate everything from capitalism to gender violence and incarceration. The illusion that some people are expendable and disposable needs to be confronted, then broken, so that we can finally get to the work of being kind and caring and joyful and really in dense and full and expansive relation with ourselves, with one another, with the earth.

And I am heartbroken about our world. So many illusions of presumed safety and security are currently collapsing under the weight of reality. The crisis in Gaza—a crisis as old as seventy-five years of occupation, displacement, and ethnic cleansing—is being felt the world over. Some are trying to hold onto ideas of Western beneficence and goodness, but all they are witnessing, all we are being forced to confront, is the violence of Western thought and practice. But we can make it against the despair of this crisis, too—if we find one another.

I am an abolitionist, and abolition means no war. I know we can and must seek the reasons violence happens, and that we must seek out the root causes that structure the cruelty under which we live. As abolitionists, we are also distinguished by our desire to avoid responding in ways that replicate or intensify these familiar violences. We seek love, not as a saccharine object or a simplistic expression of feeling good. Love means to tell the truth, love means to reckon, love means to give ceremony.

And I am here because of love. I have been deeply influenced by the Black Panther Party for Self-Defense because they help me to ask what is meant by "defense." Especially because it is said over and over again that nation-states have a right to defend themselves. But what is it, precisely, that is being defended? And what does "defense" mean? Why does "defense" mean contracts to Lockheed Martin and Northrup Grumman, and policing, and military budgets? Who is served by considering "defense" to be weapons contracts, border patrol? Can we learn from folks that exist in statelessness and have been the target of state violence? Not learning that fetishizes and celebrates being vulnerable to and the targets of violence, but to underscore the ways there is so much manifest about the human spirit and will; about our capacity to grow and expand, and to imagine and live without violent "protections" that require our submission and coerced compliance?

The Black Panther Party program included free breakfast for children, free groceries in the community, free health clinics, martial arts classes. They had guns, yes. But these practices of care, too, are defense, rooted in love, rooted in kindness, rooted in knowing that the only way to end violence is to protect our breath and becoming.

The loss of any life is an immeasurable thing. And I am heartbroken over Palestinian deaths in Gaza, in the West Bank, and other parts of occupied Palestine—deaths resulting from bombs and missiles, yes, but also from a broken healthcare system in which the majority of hospitals there have been destroyed, from the theft of clean drinking water, and from the military blockades of food shipments.

I am heartbroken because the degradation of the earth is warfare—the expulsion of white phosphorous chemicals, the killing and uprooting of olive trees, the disregard for various forms of creaturely existence. I am grieved over the targeting of doctors and nurses, of intensive care units, of pediatric facilities. Because even international law affirms that proximity to possible enemy combatants does not justify use of force that would that would imperil civilians.

I know that classrooms and universities and colleges are sites of struggle. For so many of us, we are experiencing with clarity the ways the world—so-called "out there"—has everything to do with what's happening on campuses. We are not inoculated, so we should not be unconcerned. Calls for a ceasefire as the first step, then to allow return to Palestinians that have been systematically displaced, are censored. Just as Audre Lorde says of poetry, the classroom is not a luxury, and we have to stage interventions into the violence of this world—settler colonialism, racism, Islamophobia, antisemitism, ethnonationalism—from wherever we find ourselves. And we are here. And the time to do justice, to demand otherwise, is always now.

In the religious tradition in which I grew up, we often sang songs about our collective capacity to "have the victory." Songs about overcoming difficulty and struggle and obstacles. It was not always easy to detect, how we would attain victory, but we had faith in something bigger and larger and more intense and vital than our individual selves. For me, it was (and still is) a model for how to demand justice. So I encourage you, too, to know that we will have the victory—because we already have it. Victory is not found in the capacity to wreak havoc on others, on the earth, on the water supply. Victory is not contained in the ability to coerce movement from north to south, displacement from east to west, or forced migration from communities of care and concern. Victory isn't found in military power and nuclear weapons. That kind of power is evidence of a brokenness that does not cherish the earth and its creatures as worth tending to, as worthy of care.

We have the victory because we organize and fight for life until—and even beyond—the last breath. We have victory because we find one another in chaos. We have the victory because we give and share and care and love and create friendship against imperialism, colonization, and active attempts to erase our lives, our stories. We have the victory because we understand the only world worth living in is one in which all of us can thrive. There is a profound humility to organizing, knowing that what we do and how we act may not have any appreciable impact in our lifetimes. But like water that cuts rock, it takes steady and consistent practice. And I know we can make it because you are doing that steady and consistent practice; you are modeling for us what it means to engage in struggle with integrity, with heart, with love.

I appreciate your bravery, and your courage. We need you, as the famous gospel song says, to survive.

With heart and hope and love,
Ashon

Ashon Crawley is professor of religious studies and African American and African studies at the University of Virginia. He is the author of *Blackpentecostal Breath: The Aesthetics of Possibility* (Fordham University Press, 2016) and *The Lonely Letters* (Duke University Press, 2020). His audiovisual art has been featured at Second Street Gallery, Bridge Projects, the California African American Museum, and the National Mall in Washington, DC. All his work is about otherwise possibility.

Read This if You Want to Fight Big Tech
Brian Merchant

Dear Humans,

It's a refrain so common it's rote: We live in a dystopia. The story breaks—the AI models replacing artists after ingesting their work, the driverless cars passing by someone living in theirs, the bottles of pee in a driver's van because the app penalizes lost time. We live in a dystopia. We have our work cut out for us, those of us who prefer not to.

In order to take on the chasmic inequality that defines our age, we must take on the technologies of exploitation, too. But there's a problem. For two centuries, elites have moved to mock and denigrate anyone who critiques or combats the technologies that squeeze and surveil workers as backward looking. As anti-progress. They've got a handy word for it, too—they'll call you a Luddite. I am writing you to say: let the name stick.

If you are opposed to oppressive or exploitative uses of technology in your workplace—the app that pays you less for the same ride than it does another driver, the incessant surveillance on the warehouse floor, the AI your manager is using to try to replace your job—if any of these things bother you, well, you probably are a Luddite. It's nothing to be ashamed of; quite the opposite. Two hundred years ago, in an age of inequality and technological acceleration, Luddites fought back and were hailed as working-class heroes. They were bigger than Robin Hood.

You probably have felt firsthand that we're living in another such age. As a tech reporter, I have, too. For years, I've covered powerful corporations pushing new automation technologies and extractive gig-work algorithms, even when the scales were already imbalanced against working people. I've watched as these technologies have helped push down wages, exert new levels of control, and layer oppressive digital surveillance over workers' lives. Whatever techno-optimism may have been popular a decade ago has given way to the reality of tech executives like Elon Musk embracing the far right, openly seizing state power.

But we also notice their fear: see the trend of our tech overlords buying up survival bunkers, deploying cutting-edge security details, and drafting plans to make for Mars. They insult those who might challenge them—in part because they are afraid. The real Luddites inspired fear in the industrial class and, perhaps, are a model for us to take up today.

What people remember of the Luddites, they mostly remember wrong. They might recall the caricature of agitated artisans who used a giant hammer to smash machines that automated work—but they probably do not remember that those workers had very good reasons to do that smashing. It's not your fault if you've got the Luddites wrong. Hell, I had it wrong, too. For too long, as a tech journalist, I would just blink along when a tech exec or a startup founder disparaged a critic or a disgruntled worker as a Luddite—as someone standing in the way of progress. It took reporting on Amazon's punishing working conditions, on Uber's devouring of the taxi industry and immiseration of its own workforce, to drive me to examine what Luddism was all about—to understand that they were not a punchline but working-class heroes.

For the last two hundred years, the owners of the machinery of production have had a pointed interest in keeping this mischaracterization alive. It protects their business; it insulates them from criticism, it lets them assume control over who develops technology, who it serves, and who it extracts from. No, these skilled clothworkers were not anti-technology reactionaries who sought to halt progress, or to destroy that which they did not understand; they were a fiercely organized and militant labor movement.

And what almost nobody remembers is this: the Luddites almost won.

Their campaign against the entrepreneurs and elite factory owners, and the "machinery hurtful to commonality," as one famous Luddite missive put it, brought England to the brink. By targeting the costly new technology bosses were using to drive down their wages, gain leverage over them, and degrade their working conditions, the Luddites struck back against those who were "stealing their bread." They became folk heroes in the process. Clothworkers tried for a decade to get laws passed that would provide minimum wages and protections from automation; they were laughed out of Parliament. Taking up the hammers was a tactic of last resort.

In doing so, the Luddites won the hearts and minds of England's nascent working class, earned the admiration of Lord Byron, and inspired solidarity among steelworkers, shoemakers, colliers, and tradesmen far afield of the cloth industry—poets wrote hymns about them, and sympathetic officials looked on as they smashed the machinery of inequality.

So the British monarchy did what many elites tend to do when they are threatened by the interests of working people: they used force. The prince regent's government deployed a force larger than the one it had sent abroad to fight Napoleon to combat the Luddites; by some counts, it was the single biggest domestic occupation in English history. Tens of thousands of troops, militia, and mercenaries were deployed to the front lines of the Industrial Revolution. British Parliament, in the throes of what the historian Eric Hobsbawm called its "most ferociously conservative" period, made breaking machinery a crime punishable by death. The state sent spies to infiltrate Luddite meetings.

It took a bloody state reprisal, in which dozens of working men, women, and children were shot, beaten, or hung to death, to extinguish the Luddites' flame. And that flame has to be kept free of oxygen, lest workers get too comfortable with the idea of criticizing, protesting, resisting—or even sabotaging—the technologies that enable bosses to surveil and degrade them.

Because this is something else that is little remembered about the Luddites: they did not lose out because their views were less popular, or because their goods couldn't compete in a marketplace with automated production. They lost because they were systematically crushed by the state and an ascendant class of entrepreneurial elite, who wanted nothing more than to use technology to profit the rich at the expense of working people.

In their defeat, however, the Luddites did not reveal, as many are still mistakenly led to believe, the weakness of their position. They revealed their power. But the Luddites commanded such power, threatened the elite of England so wholly, that it took the full wrath of the British state to turn them, and their ideas, away. And they couldn't even do it, not completely: the Luddites may have lost the war over their material conditions, but they won some key victories in the long game. They helped crystallize a working-class consciousness in England; they paved the road to reform that legalized unions; they inspired Mary Shelley's *Frankenstein*, and laid the groundwork for two hundred years of social and cultural resistance to reckless or exploitative technologies.

They mattered more than they ever might have known in their own time.

And that's what I hope to impart, above all, onto the new generation of Luddites, whether they adopt the name or not. Those who may be organizing against a boss who hopes to replace their jobs with the output of a large language model operated by OpenAI, who may be one of the tens of thousands of gig workers rising in opposition to Uber's increasingly draconian practices, who may be pushing back against Amazon and fighting for union recognition. They may call us backward, or hopeless; they may try to insult us; they may call us Luddites.

To which we should say: Good. There is power in being a Luddite. In refusing to be dominated by technology designed to serve bosses at our expense. In demanding a seat at the table when it is determined how such technologies are developed and deployed. We saw that power in the strikes by the Writers Guild of America and the Screen Actors Guild in 2023: a key contention was over whether or not the studios could use AI systems to displace the work of writers and actors.

By drawing a red line and rejecting the use of a technology that would be used to exploit them, the writers revived the tactic of Luddism in the twenty-first century. And it worked. The American public, anxious about the encroachment of managers' AI into their own lives, supported the writers over their studio bosses by stunning margins.

Other workers have embraced the politics of refusal, too. Illustrators like Molly Crabapple and the Center for Artistic Inquiry and Reporting have called for bans on the use of generative AI in editorial outlets. Artists, authors, and actors have brought class action lawsuits against AI companies like OpenAI and tech giants like Google and Meta for harvesting and profiting off of their work without their consent. In California, the Teamsters are rejecting fully automated trucking. We must recognize the power and potential in the refusal of the technologies of dominion that threaten so many of us, and we must embrace it.

Today, we have tools beyond the hammer. We have collective bargaining; the original Luddites did not, because it was outlawed. However much beleaguered and conditional to the current administration, we have—for now—the protections of the National Labor Relations Board; the original Luddites did not, as England was still a functioning monarchy. We hold the symbolic power of that hammer, to refuse, to oppose, to dismantle.

The machinery that elites use to hold dominion over working people is, as ever, more brittle than they would like us to believe. Take generative AI. It's unpopular, for one—a source of anxiety among the working class, who recognize the ways managers might use it to squeeze them, and a source of scorn among Gen Z tastemakers, who see its output as unethical and uncool. It's also immensely resource intensive, requiring tons of compute power, skilled labor, and energy to run. Critics argue the AI bubble is a house of cards; stalwart resistance may help bring it down. Organizers everywhere should not hesitate to target technologies being deployed by managers to replace workers' tasks, surveil them, or degrade their working conditions; these can be catalysts for great solidarity. We must support groups like Gig Workers Rising, the Amazon Labor Union, and the African Content Moderators Union—after all, much of modern technology is made possible only by workers who Big Tech tries to make invisible—in their struggles to improve their own working conditions, and all of ours.

As oppressive as such machinery can seem, as total as Silicon Valley's power might appear, it's crucial we never forget the lesson of the Luddites: machinery can always be refused. And failing that, it can be broken.

Sincerely,
Brian

Brian Merchant is a journalist and author who covers technology, labor, and politics. He is a reporter in residence at the AI Now Institute and was the technology columnist at the *Los Angeles Times*. He is the author of *Blood in the Machine: The Origins of the Rebellion against Big Tech* (Little, Brown, & Co., 2023) and cofounder of VICE's speculative fiction outlet *Terraform*. His newsletter is BloodintheMachine.com.

Read This if You're Hurting and Want to Find Your People

Ash Williams

Dear Sibling in Struggle,

 In the safety and comfort of intimate space with other queer and trans folks over the past twelve years, my chosen family and I talk about how we are all facing moments of uninterrupted grief. We talk about the overwhelm of climate disasters, the continued persecution and repression of protestors, and attacks against the ways we choose to live our lives. We are living in some wild-ass times. This moment might have you feeling like you have to be everywhere, be everything to everyone. I felt that way once, too.

 While this chaotically unfolding moment might have you feeling like you have to be on every front, I want to remind you that this is absolutely the time to pause, batten down the hatches, and figure out where and how we fit in with what we have to offer. I started organizing as an undergraduate, alongside other students at the University of North Carolina, both on and off campus. On campus, I fought against cuts to funding for the university's cultural centers, as well as tuition increases, the hiring of the infamous, debt-collecting Margaret Spellings as president, and harmful policies impacting transgender students, faculty, and staff. Off campus, I became involved in organizing with other queer and trans people to address violence against the local Black trans community. During this time, we used direct action and political education to organize and mobilize people against NC HB2, the notorious "bathroom bill" that sought to, among other things, ban trans people from using bathrooms of their choice. In addition to that work, I became heavily involved with organizing alongside immigrant and refugee communities against the police and Immigration and Customs Enforcement (ICE). The curiosities I have around transforming emotions into action grew as I organized funeral processions, vigils, rallies, protests, and teach-ins for community members to learn from each other, process anger and loss, and practice solidarity. I began to realize there is something unique about the spaces created by bodies who are activated by a particular set of emotions. People often left those actions feeling ready to learn and do more. From there, I also became introduced to the tactic, practice, and study of nonviolent direct action. Practicing direct action as a way of life and collaborating with other disabled, queer, and principled folks led me to front lines near and far. Working across movements has always been something central to my work as an organizer and a doula.

When I had my first abortion eight years ago, I never could have imagined the immense impact it would have on my life, my organizing, and my relationship to struggling for bodily autonomy. The year was 2016. I was finishing my master's program in philosophy. I was teaching dance, selling jeans, and working as a research and graduate assistant to pay my and my partner's bills. I was uninsured. Outside of school and work, I was involved with a ragtag group of trans and queer radicals and students who fought back against police brutality and violence against trans and queer folks, and bailed people out of jail. I was in a dead-end relationship with a cis partner who was abusive. When I learned I was pregnant, I knew I did not want to be. I was upset at myself and felt distraught for a while. I knew abortion was a thing, but I didn't know a lot about it. I knew it was costly, and I knew that it wasn't covered by health insurance (even if I had been insured). I was sure I wanted to have an abortion and choose myself, but I couldn't have foreseen that having an abortion would be one of the most important direct actions of my life.

I remember preparing to tell a close friend about wanting to have an abortion. I felt sure she would be supportive. She was someone who I had confided in all throughout school. We knew each other well, and I felt like I could share anything with her without feeling ashamed. I mustered up the confidence to tell her I knew what I wanted to do about being pregnant. When I told her that I wanted to have an abortion, she responded by telling me that I was taking the easy way out. She was not supportive. I felt blamed, shamed, and shocked that I was receiving so much negativity from someone who I thought knew me. I looked elsewhere for support. I turned to my trans and queer organizing friends who held me with love and support. Those folks supported my decision and even helped me pay for my first abortion.

One of those folks—a white girl named Grace—drove me to my appointment. She waited for me. She fed me immediately after my abortion, and when she learned that my iron was low, she cooked me collard greens and stayed at my house with me. She was my abortion doula before I even knew what that was. Experiencing community members loving on me after my first abortion had a profound impact on me.

I knew that if getting an abortion was challenging for me, it had to be more challenging for folks with even less than I had. I could not afford to pay for my abortions on my own, and I relied financially on people who trusted me to make the decision for myself, as well as on my local abortion fund. My experience was not easy. I experienced being misgendered and deadnamed throughout my abortion experiences, and even after advocating for myself, it didn't seem to make a difference. I didn't receive care that truly took into account my entire being and person. Pregnant people who are considering abortion are often navigating other important events in their lives, and considering or having an abortion doesn't mean that the other parts of your life can be put on hold. For me, it was no different. I was navigating intimate partner violence, and throughout my abortion experience, I did not feel like I had space to name that. Adding onto all these other pressures, when I arrived at both of my procedural abortion appointments, I was met with police presence, anti-abortion protestors begging me not to go through with it, and, thankfully, smiles from pro-abortion clinic escorts. I would not have made it through the experience without my friends and pro-abortion advocates, and I am so grateful that I did.

My experience led me to thinking about what I might have to offer others in similar situations. After my first abortion, I learned more about using abortion storytelling to combat stigma and shame. I shared my story with anyone who would listen. I hoped offering my experience would shed light on what it's like for other Black trans people who can't afford to pay for their abortions on their own, who need more support. Because I was so vocal about my experience of abortion, people found their way to me. People began to share their experiences with me and ask me to help them access abortion. It started with folks in North Carolina, but that quickly expanded beyond the state as I made myself more available to people further away. I continue to be guided and grounded by what was missing from my abortion experience as I show up for others as an abortion doula. Not only did I become laser focused on increasing abortion access through storytelling, advocacy, and fundraising, but I began to connect the issue of waning abortion access to the other justice issues that matter to me. I also saw the limits of narrowly focusing on abortion access as I connected the work of women of color (both pre- and post-*Roe*) to struggles to realize a future world where every person has what they need to be able to make decisions for themselves and their families in all areas of their life.

I am grateful to have first encountered the reproductive justice framework during the formative time that I did. The Reproductive Justice framework challenges us to engage with the ambitious idea that we all deserve to live free from harm. In my own work, I consider what it might take to achieve that freedom amid the hyper-criminalization of the current moment. Bringing me back to a cross-movement analysis, the third principle of the

RJ framework connects struggles to stop cop cities to the fight to decriminalize abortion to resistance against the anti-trans legislation sweeping with hurricane force through the Southeast. These experiences as a community organizer and an abortion doula impelled me to understand my skills more clearly and figure out the best ways I can use what I have to improve material conditions, and to create paradigmatic shifts in how we understand the effects of criminalization and colonization on our communities and our bodies. I wondered: How can I convey the interconnectedness of these movements and frameworks?

In 2020, at the start of the global pandemic, I was presented with an opportunity to plug in with other abortion doulas living in Western North Carolina. Together, we gave new life to a preexisting full-spectrum doula collective. We transformed the collective into a formal abortion doula collective, focused on offering free, non-judgmental, gender-affirming, comprehensive abortion care. This was also a time when I was recognizing my own needs as an underemployed survivor of intimate partner violence, and as someone on probation who could no longer be everywhere but was still determined to keep showing up for the people around me. Even on probation, my work didn't pause or stop, but I found more creative, less visible ways of supporting abortion seekers. I had already stopped trying to be everything to everyone, and I knew I had to refocus and ground myself in my needs and those of people in my community. It was not only people who know me but also complete strangers who looked out for me, making sure I had the necessary support to make it through my probationary sentence and keep doing my work as an abortion doula. Today, we continue to hold down the Mountain Area Abortion Doula Collective, which provides abortion support to folks all over, but primarily in the South.

My experience and training led me to be more mindful about how I advocate for the decriminalization of abortion and increased access—by fighting to keep existing clinics open, helping people get to their appointments, and not complying with the law.

I have always had a soft spot for fundraising for urgent causes, like swerving evictions, paying money to help people get released from spaces of incarceration, and helping people with health care expenses. For years, I've helped people fund their own abortions by using my personal networks and my social media platforms to encourage others to donate to "make their abortion dreams a reality." I enjoy supporting people who have fallen through the cracks of non-profit funding mechanisms. I work diligently to fund abortions for people so that they can focus on a different part of their experience. They don't usually have a lot of time to make many considerations. In addition to funding abortions, I have coordinated transportation for folks who need to leave their home state to travel to access care. I've connected countless folks to people who can offer emotional, physical, logistical, and informational support where they live. I recently funded an abortion for a friend who lives with their parents and needed a safe place to go after leaving the clinic for their procedural abortion. I funded the abortion, and I was able to raise enough funds for them to have a place to stay after their abortion that was not their home.

Abortion doulas work with other types of care workers to offer support. We work with radical mental health and health care workers, spiritualists, artists, teachers, students, abortion funds, movement attorneys, and affinity groups to increase access to abortion care in our communities. Last year, I worked with LGBTQ domestic violence specialists to relocate some experiencing intimate partner violence and an abortion. I've cared for patients in abortion clinics, and I have built relationships with clinic workers so as to improve the lives of patients needing gender-affirming care. It is the strong network of care that makes it possible for me to do my work, and it is my ability to sit with someone and be with them through a difficult and increasingly criminalized experience that tells me I am in the right place.

As I continue to show up for folks, I am also pausing. I am allowing myself not to get on every call, to be in every Signal group, to attend every meeting, or to read every headline. I pause so I can remain grounded in my purpose and where my skills are steadfast. I am battening down the hatches by checking in about the cultures of security that surround my life and work—for instance, by having more conversations with my affinity group about what the fuck we're going to do about the increased scrutiny placed on abortion seekers and community providers, and by divesting from platforms like Google. For now, I am feeling content with what I can do to show up for myself and my folks right now. I feel encouraged by those around me who continue to provide critical care in the community. Finally, I am affirmed by the righteous Black midwives, death workers, doulas, activists, organizers, and abortion storytellers who came before me. My relationships with the dead allow me to keep showing up for the people who are still here.

Given where we have been, and where it seems like things are headed, here's what I can tell you about how to keep moving forward: keep nurturing the relationships you've been building over the past few years. Figure out where and with whom you feel poured into. Think about what you have to offer others. So much more will be required from us in this time, but I think this is a generative starting place.

With care,
Ash

Ash Williams (he/him) is a Black trans abortion doula, community organizer, and death worker from Fayetteville, North Carolina.

Read This if You're Disabled and Trying to Figure Things Out

Leah Lakshmi Piepzna-Samarasinha and Jane Shi

Dear You,

    Leah: We know. You feel like you're the only one talking about disability. You blink as you watch people read disabled books but run meetings where noone masks. Or, despite all our work, you realize that they live in a world without disabled arts, politics, culture, people. You're so fucking tired and spooned out, and yet there you are, doing all the crip everything.

    Or: all the disabled people you know are at war with each other. There is so much inter-community conflict, pain, and misunderstanding. There are five of you, and you are all trying to do collective care for each other. You are both regularly imperfect, and sometimes one or more of you does something extra hectic. There are white disableds who take up a lot of space who are annoying, to put it mildly, who think disability justice was invented for them to be leaders or define what it is or have everyone take care of their needs in a 24/7, one-way concierge service. There are BIPOC who don't say "the D word," and you get it, but it's been years and it's hard to build when people are still in (understandable) crip shame. You are the bridge, holding all the shit up and connecting it with your back brace.

    Jane: You're tired. Bridges need care, and all the money that should be going into bridge maintenance is going into policing. You are building yourself as others cross you, and you look both ways to check if the rope is tied tight enough to hold others, let alone yourself. When textbooks and policies say to leave the old and disabled behind during a tsunami, becoming your own infrastructure as a disabled person seems inevitable. Do you have to rebuild science, medicine, and technology too? When you plant Dr. Refaat Alareer's poem on the side of the Burrard Bridge, on the occupied territories of the Musqueam, Squamish, and Tsleil-Waututh peoples in so-called Vancouver, you're stopping traffic with a group. You peer at your friend in the distance and feel hopeful. You're reminded that your peers leading environmental movements are learning about disability; they care. But on days when you can't leave your bed, your heart an impenetrable cloud, your inbox full of emails demanding to segregate immunocompromised and disabled people (Mandatory masking from 2:00 p.m. to 3:00 p.m. only! Community event up fourteen flights of stairs!), you wish there was one more hour in the day when you didn't have to fight.

Leah: You're tired of this bullshit. Why are the most tired disabled ones still doing all the work? Where is the disabled future already? Will you die, get forgotten, or burn out extra hard?

Jane: It's 2024, 2025, 2026, 2027 . . . and it feels like you've been alone in your room for years, seasons passing as gracelessly as minutes, as seconds, the markings for the passage of time losing meaning, becoming grating. The word "community," too, sometimes feels like a slap in the face. Where is everyone? And perhaps more embarrassing, more difficult to admit, is that you are angry that community feels hard, in a way that is so autistic, so complex-trauma survivor, so specific to you. The more accurate word, "communities," fails to address or offer balm for the breakdown, the abandonment, and the specific shame that accompanies being deliberately isolated and abandoned. And yes, the specific shame and abandonment that feels so personal, targeted, is not from strangers you've never met but from people you care about and love and admire and wish you had communicated with better.

Why was the Freedom Convoy (which in 2022 protested the Canadian government's vaccine mandate and occupied the city of Ottawa in the style of the January 6th Capitol attack) the only time nondisabled people you know spoke out about anti-vaxxers, anti-maskers? What do you do when you can't read about COVID anymore? What do you do when you get flashbacks when entering disabled and nondisabled movement spaces alike, especially ones where everything feels urgent, where everyone is needed, where everyone is in crisis or dying? What do you do when asking for help feels painful—not because you don't understand, intellectually, the power and importance of interdependence, but because the memory of being taken advantage of in your deepest moments of crises eclipses the new muscle memories you built, for giving yourself grace or the gift of letting others in?

Reader, these are all feelings you should get to feel, questions you should get to ask, in the moments between speaking up, organizing, writing, strengthening relationships, making mistakes, having conflicts, telling the truth, telling yourself white lies that you rest enough, caring for others, or caring for yourself. After all, every part of you matters and should get its turn to speak.

Jane: The Encrypted Passcode to the Heart's Safety Deposit Box

A little more than a decade ago, at twenty-one, after I was prescribed antidepressants and diagnosed with depression, I wrote a Facebook post about being disabled. While at the time, I needed the prompting of a doctor and institutional accommodations to "permit" me to claim a disabled experience, this pronouncement was also my way of reclaiming agency and a desire to live free from the violence of ableist abuse. Over time, I realized ableism was central to much of my life experiences, and that disability justice is a movement indispensable to my own and others' liberation. Over time, I realized I had been disabled my whole life.

At my English honors literature program at university, I was an easy target. Blurting things out at the wrong times, not being already familiar with the white British canon, and, perhaps worst of all, not knowing how to be a social creature among the other twenty-year-old students, I threw off the equilibrium of the classroom just by being me: a queer, racialized, and neurodivergent immigrant grappling with obvious-to-me-now symptoms of complex post-traumatic stress and the confusion of being a young person at a big neoliberal university.

Being bookish and loving language was not enough to thrive; I had to learn to camouflage—as in, hide my autistic, neurodivergent traits—so that in between coming up with something clever to say about Virginia Woolf's *The Waves*, I could dodge biting remarks from my classmates. (Reader, I was not good at dodging them.) These, combined with sexual harassment and relentless social humiliation, made every class feel like a cruel improv session involving metaphorical dodgeballs and literal critical theory.

After taking too many caffeine pills one winter semester, my bodymind rebelled with a less easy-to-ignore depression. I couldn't put on clothes on my own or fathom completing my coursework on existentialist philosophy or African American literature (taught by a white man). I yearned for a new way to be in the world. I was dissatisfied from reading texts on materiality and structures, and I felt, despite my love of books and literature, that literary criticism in the academy did not change the material conditions or structures around me. At the back of my heart, I also wanted to know why I was so easy to pick on. I wanted to change the conditions of my life.

So, I took a gap year and joined housing marches and did anti-violence work through a local organization. I learned about disability justice at a workshop the organization held. I attended Idle No More marches. I learned about Palestine; I learned that movements can be a dangerous place when you are young, queer, racialized, and have your heart laying outside of its safety deposit box. In the 2010s, Yahoo hadn't bought Tumblr yet. I was craving mentorship, community, a sense of being at home, a sense of kinship, a sense of safety in found families that I couldn't find at university or in my family of origin.

People become organizers and activists because they are hungry for belonging. People become care workers because they have not been cared for in the ways they should have been. We agitate because our survival depends on it. We also come to organizing with real fear in our hearts, inherited violence, and a dangerous sense of scarcity that morphs into a desire for power and maintaining the status quo. In my short time as an organizer, I have learned that it is easier to call out others' behavior than to change one's own; that for many of us, it is far, far easier to take care of others and take on others' pain than to attend to our own. I have learned that there are no saviors or heroes in movements, just people who show up.

One of the biggest fears I had growing up, on par with heights, was becoming homeless. I knew, instinctively but without the words for it, that what I was so terrified of was not merely the cold of the concrete and of rain-drenched skin, but of the humiliation of having nowhere to go, of having to rely on dangerous people, of losing my belongings, of a disabled and mad poverty that generations in my family experienced in an unrecorded but somatically palpable way. When I began to unravel and examine this fear, I realized that I was also struggling to imagine myself being wanted, cared for—not just physically and materially with a roof over my head, but also emotionally, valued for who I am regardless of what I could produce or do for others.

There was no utopia waiting for me in organizing spaces. Nor, I realized over time, was there in found families built within disabled, mad, and neurodivergent QTIBIPOC communities. Like most people who escape their first oppressors, be they family, academia, or a hostile society, I found new ways to be hurt and new ways to hurt others in these alternative family structures. Despite world-shattering and ever-proliferating betrayals, I kept searching, waiting, searching. I wrote poetry. I organized my own shit. I shit-talked until I had no one else to shit-talk to but the mirror. What I did find in that searching has been quieter, more internal, more about what to do with the heart.

Today, I see myself in so many other young, queer disability justice organizers who find ourselves banging our heads against the brick wall of ableism, racism, and state violence, and who feel both an immense sense of anomie and a strong desire to connect, love, and find elders and kin—real elders who could take us under their wing, real kin around whom we can be our real selves and bare our rawest, most inconvenient emotions. If I didn't find my people in a sick and disabled people of color Facebook group or in arts non-profits with the most radical branding or at an action, where did I find them? The truth is: I found them when I decided, again and again, that I was worth fighting for; that I wasn't a footnote in the story of my life; that I was the person I wanted to become; that is, I was the only person I'll ever become. I had to choose for myself, over and over, that I wanted to grow, and I wanted others to grow with, make mistakes around, and to trust that they will be there for me and be honest with me in my loneliest hour just as much as I would be there for them.

Grace Lee Boggs once shared, as would my father, that "we have to change ourselves in order to change the world." When I was twenty-one, my father abruptly disclosed, as though neither he nor I had been ready before, that he was a student leader in the June 4, 1989, protests in Nanjing, Jiangsu, and was subsequently blacklisted from career opportunities by the Chinese government. This is why, he told me, our family came to this country in the late '90s. In a talk from Larissa Lai on her book *The Lost Century*, she speaks about how silence can be a form of protection from trauma for the next generation. The bodymind holds the secrets of time and acts accordingly, like those who came before me did when they disclosed in the form of lessons, in the form of habits, in the form of flaws. If our silence won't protect us, as Audre Lorde would say, why do some silences get broken while others persist?

I want to organize from a place of care, abundance, and discernment. I suspect that the state repression my father's generation experienced crushed their spirits, but in telling me this story, he reminded me that I've inherited a need to demand more for our lives. I learn, too, from what he didn't share: that he felt abandoned and alone, that he was struggling to juggle being the head of the household of his new immigrant family while acquiring new diagnoses and physical injuries, feeling (wrongly) that he had no place but me to lodge his anger and grief.

    Disability justice is a movement that recognizes the need to tend to the spirit. It moves us to listen to our grief. Disability justice sees my disabled family's desire to cling onto the respectability of the Western nuclear family as a response to generational trauma; it offers me a way to seek out modes of care and resistance that lie beyond these limits. Disability justice isn't an abstract movement that can be argued or intellectualized into being, that nonprofits and corporations and academia can co-opt; it's something we practice every day with one another and with ourselves; the very models of leadership and education that the nondisabled and white disability rights world cherish and idolize do not hold the same water.

    It is important that we continue to refuse these models with our loved ones and with ourselves, and imagine disability justice as everyone's responsibility, for everyone to learn from and practice. Because the stakes are just that high. In an interview I did with Rita Wong, she shared something from another poet, the late Claire Harris, that sticks with me still: to identify as an activist and to allow ourselves to be called activists is to suggest that liberation is relegated to the work of a few, not everyone. This insight helps me recognize my father's role in revolution and make sense of mine. To search is to open ourselves up to change.

    This is not to say that organizing and movement work don't require specific skills that take time and practice to hone, with the support of teachers, or that those without lived experiences should get to barge into the room unannounced with unsolicited opinions, but to imagine the distribution of movement work as truly liberatory: that we each have a role to play, and that it's okay that it takes several tries for us to find the one that fits snugly for us; that taking years to rest, then coming back, is more than welcome when our bodyminds and lives require it of us; that doing something is better than the corrosive stillness of despair.

In a tweet, poet and writer Cyrée Jarelle Johnson once alluded to newer generations of disability justice organizers paving the way of the movement and honing its directions. This insight recognizes young people's agency and the importance of disagreement and conflict, and working through them; of invention, reinvention, and building something new; of adapting to the present and breaking cycles we didn't know we needed to break. Disability justice is inseparable from youth liberation and undoing the violence of colonization—the specific spiritual violence that makes us feel that we are not part of the universe and that our wisdom isn't enough or wanted.

You are part of the universe, and your wisdom is wanted. Your guts, your heart, your mitochondria that remembers the air fifty generations ago—your everything.

As babies and elders and everyone in between face catastrophic levels of devastation from eugenicist policies, climate catastrophe, and settler colonial violence, tending to our spirits is vital. For me, it helps to reach into my childhood understanding of a spiritual self, creating space for wonder, care, trust, and compassion. It helps to ask myself what it means to let go of white, Western, abled understandings of "goodness" as a moral imperative and instead imagine justice as the action that creates freedom. So much of this work is internal, and so much of this work cannot be done without others, without relationships that make you forget (however momentarily) that you ever felt unlovable and unworthy.

Doing something with others to change things, the simplest definition I have for movement work, requires an act of faith. It requires gathering your Fear, Anxiety, Guilt, Rage, Shame, and Grief in a room and saying, "You all have a role here." And saying, "Here's Faith too. She's new here. Let's welcome her in. Let's listen to what she has to say." It is hard to find your people right away, out there, what with all the noise, false advertising, conflicts of interest, misunderstandings, heartbreaks, abuse of power, and capitalism. It will take several tries. But if all else fails, you'll still have your various parts. You'll still have you, the you that still loves you, the you that wants to live despite all the odds.

Life has taught me to create a passcode for the safety deposit box within which my heart has learned to find comfort and stability. Exhaustion has taught me to write the passcode down. The double-edged sword that is our disabled lives on the internet has taught me to put the passcode in an encrypted file (literally, figuratively). Acts of faith help me give the link to one or two (or more) people also yearning for disability justice futures, for liberation, for a better world. Or simply someone you love and want to continue loving.

Just as I will never know if the yarrow seeds I scattered on a lawn across a bank will sprout in a few months or next spring, just as my father will never know what he sparked for future generations when he stepped forward as a leader back in 1989, we will never fully know what our acts of faith will conjure up. But change is not about knowing, immediate results, or even forgetting our fear, doubt, and uncertainty. Conjuring is magical, inexplicable, like the earth and the solar system, like the capacity for our neural pathways to rewire.

The heart, like you, yearns to move and be still, at an even rhythm. And if it's not even, because COVID gave you heart palpitations, it still yearns for quiet and to be held. Who will you send your links to? What will you build with each other's hearts? You can always change the passcode. And when you're ready, open the latch again.

Sincerely,
Jane

Leah: A bb Illder Speaking to the Illders, the Youngers, and the Others (Basically, Everyone)

I still feel like the new kid when it comes to disability justice (DJ). It feels like yesterday that I was wide eyed, sitting in my first Sins Invalid meeting in 2009, having my mind blown by older crips who said what they needed in the access check-in simply and without apology.

2009 feels like five minutes ago, but it was a decade and a half. Since then, my worlds/our worlds have turned over and transformed over and over again. I am forty-nine, turning fifty next year. I finally accept it when people refer to me as a bb illder—even though, now more than ever, I know that being an elder is a verb, a process, not automatic, a work in progress, a status earned that one must maintain. I did not quite know it would feel so unknown—to survive to now, to live to a cripple middle age as a person and a movement worker, and still not know how to inhabit it. I did not know that it would feel so lonely.

I fought to stay here, to live, to not kill myself or be taken out. I still do. I did not know that successfully fighting a battle to survive would mean outliving so many people I love. People who were both friends and comrades, that sweet spot of both that my friend Max Airborne spoke of in a recent social media post. We were alone, and we fought to find our way to each other. Sometimes we continue. And, yes, I talk to my ancestors in the spirit realm, though I wish they were corporeal on my porch.

Even if I don't have a slew of illders illder to me to tell me how to do this, I have my knowledge from being a younger and a 30s both schooled and dismayed by many kinds of elders. I know that I do not have all the answers, and I resist calls that insist I must. I know that there's something to my thirty-ish years of memory and experience in the movement—that I have some earned skills, respect, and leadership, and above all history and memory—but it doesn't mean I'm always right. I know it is an act of subversion to ableist patriarchy to act like my older crip queer brown body is valuable, not a throw-away grossness now that I am not younger and striving to "keep up."

I know that knowledge is not transactional and is not a one-way street. I learn from people older, younger, and of similar age to me. Crip and ND age is different. Folks younger than me are quasars shining light and dark, show me things I never would have thought of. I cherish the ones illder to me, even when I disagree with them or they are harmful or fuck up, for showing me the way not to be. Some of us younger than us live "older" sooner, because of a sense that they may not have an average lifespan. Some of us who make it to older have knowledge we all need to practice that most quoted, least understood principle of DJ: sustainability. To be a crip is to be a time traveler, to understand quantum time—that we move through time, more than many.

What is some of the memory knowledge I carry from being in this movement for fifteen years, for twenty-seven-ish years before it used the phrase "DJ"?

I remember when it felt like there were only twenty of us who used the term "DJ" in North America—because there were. I remember what it felt like to be in the small, new, hot, atomic beginning of ideas that would catch fire. I remember that early blissful movement high space where we started. And I remember what it felt like the first time my heart broke in DJ, where that circle got shattered for a moment and people were still coming to me, all the new crips who needed this movement or knowledge so badly, to saying they'd read the blog post of someone in leadership who was brilliant and who I also knew privately had done wrong. I remember the feeling of not knowing what to do.

I skip forward from those moments to what I knew then, what I learned, what I still know and see: We don't automatically know how to love ourselves, or each other, as disabled people—it is a lifetime commitment and process. Let alone know how to work together. I mean, we do: often we come together and it is magic and seamless. And what is also true is the cliff of not knowing each other's languages and needs because often we barely know our own.

What I believe, and want to share, is that this doesn't have to mean betrayal. Maybe now that there are thousands of us, there is more room to take a breath, know this crip is not one of only five in the world, to know that saying, "hey that hurt," or "didn't work," doesn't mean someone is being thrown off the life raft. We also don't all like each other, get along, or jibe with each other's personalities. We don't need to do that to fight for our freedom.

We still lack enough places to struggle through political questions, gain education, argue in a principled way. But I believe we can develop them, and that we can have a diversity of tactics without our differences being equated to personal betrayal. It's not easy. The times keep being a constantly banging gong of disaster. Who has time to have a Rigorous Space of Political Study and Disagreement? And yet, don't we? When you come over to my porch and hit your one-hitter, and we eat halal cart and shoot the shit, and every other sentence starts with "Sorry, but I'm choosing violence," or "I know, I'm talking shit but . . ." and you blew your one spoon for a social on me, I'm honored. We both need it so bad.

That's where I land, I guess. On three things. One, to trail from above: find your people. The three crips you Zoom co-work with on Friday, your regularly scheduled couch Facetime, the homie you voice memo to voice memo to, the six people who wear masks and come over to your yard to just kick it and shoot the shit. You need it; we need us. I almost died living someplace with clean air and water and cheap rent; because I didn't have it. I didn't know when I started I would need so much space to hold the grief—not just from the people I love who are gone, but from movement losses and betrayals, the "This is Disability Justice" unauthorized biography, *Behind the Music* shit that pops up like "You remember that moment in 2015?" or whatever. What holds me, and keeps me in, and makes my life possible and worth living is this shit: watching YouTubes with a freak genius on Discord at 1:00 a.m., talking through hard shit we don't know the answer to when we're supposed to be co-working, going to an outdoor rave for thirty minutes when we're supposed to be resting. We always do our best work at the wrong unscheduled time.

Finally, I want to circle back to the: sometimes you just don't know what to do. And it doesn't mean you're a failure—to the person, the situation, or the movement. Sometimes there is nothing to do. Sometimes doing nothing is the best option. Just because you're a Mad cripple genius, like Sherlock or Watson but BIPOC, and you can crip the elementary solution to a problem that has all the ableds scratching their heads, sometimes you get handed a cripple calculus problem you just can't answer. I know everything looks like and is a banging gong of emergency, you crip FEMA, but sometimes you will hit a wall of: don't know. Let it rock. Sit with it. See what emerges.

Finally, finally: you are worth more than your amazing fix-it capabilities. You are not valued solely for your care genius. If all you did was sit and shit and breathe for the rest of your life and laugh at a meme, you would have value. Sometimes, even when we don't believe in supercripdom, we use it, or get pressured to use it, to redeem ourselves. To ourselves, to "the movement," the world. See, Ma, I may be disabled, but look at all this organizing I'm doing. I've been there, done that. I've witnessed people I love go into the movement because they were Crazy or disabled, then get told, explicitly or implicitly, "you're an organizer. No more surprise ICU stays or grippy sock vacations are allowed for you. You are a disability justice organizer; you don't get to be disabled or nuts anymore." That one hurts my heart so bad. No. Fight against it. We have to make movements where our hospital stays and bad days still happen. Make them, for you, for the others, for us. Write me and tell me how it's going?

Oh yeah—take time off. Smoke your weed, go to the lake, make tea and be on the couch all weekend. I'll join you.

Yours in love and struggle, as we persist,
Leah

Jane Shi is a poet, writer, and organizer living on the occupied, stolen, and unceded territories of the xʷməθkʷəy̓əm (Musqueam), Skwxwú7mesh (Squamish), and səlililw̓ətaʔɬ (Tsleil-Waututh) peoples. Her debut poetry collection is *echolalia echolalia* (Brick Books, 2024). She wants to live in a world where love is not a limited resource, land is not mined, hearts are not filched, and bodies are not violated.

Read This if You Are Fighting Deportations and You're Afraid or Discouraged

Aly Wane

Dear Immigration Organizer,

    The battle for social justice toward repair is a long, intergenerational one. And as an immigration activist, you know this as well as anyone. You have seen immigration and border patrol agents rip families apart, threaten immigrants and citizens alike, and incarcerate and deport countless people. Worse, you have seen too many of your neighbors either look the other way or, in this fascist atmosphere, approve of this mass cruelty. It takes a toll and is incredibly demoralizing and destabilizing.

    The Trump era is a serious escalation of a xenophobic logic adopted by both major parties. This president has been more than happy to exploit the global wave of xenophobia that has accompanied the failures of the neoliberal era. As the manic logic of markets has taken over, so has inequality risen to unprecedented levels. And whenever inequality rises, anti-immigrant politics are sure to follow. This is a global problem.

    I share the frustrations and fears associated with this era, but it is important to understand that this repression is nothing new. It is just a concentrated escalation of what has been happening for a long time.

    All of this is personal to me. I haven't had the luxury of looking at this crisis at a remove.

    I was brought to the US as a nine-year-old child on a diplomatic visa because my mom got a job at the United

Nations in New York City. I changed my immigration status to a student visa by the end of high school, but that visa expired in 1996 when, two years into my studies at the University of Pennsylvania, I could no longer afford to go to school. Though I had been in the country since 1985, neither of my visa statuses counted toward a Green Card or any path to citizenship. Like many immigrants, I was stuck in a legal labyrinth with no exit. One of the open secrets of the immigration battle is that while both major parties have continually agreed on ever-increasing levels of enforcement, they have offered few paths to legalization. Organizing became my salvation, especially after the cataclysm of 9/11. I realized then that my life as an immigrant had changed, and that the so-called War on Terror abroad would be manifested as a war on immigrants domestically. In that atmosphere, every immigrant instantly became suspect, and "illegal alien" became synonymous with "potential terrorist" in the hegemonic political narrative.

Though scared about my status, I threw myself into political activist life and found some people working with the Chicago branch of the American Friends Service Committee who agreed to hire me despite my status. Back then, I focused on anti-war and anti-globalization issues, analyzing and critiquing the neocolonialist nature of modern capitalism and its impact on the African continent. Little did I know that this work would greatly inform my organizing on immigration.

First, however, I had to face my fears. Like most undocumented folks, I was terrified of anyone finding out about my status, so I did not want to organize on the issue. But eventually, the issue found me. I live in Syracuse, New York, a city one hundred miles from the northern border, which gives Customs and Border Protection (CBP) jurisdiction. In the mid 2000s, some of us started hearing awful stories about immigrants being disappeared from the streets. Quickly enough, we figured out that immigration agents were using racial profiling and snatching people up. We got together and formed a group called the Detention Task Force to bail out immigrants caught in the dragnet, and we started on anti-deportation work.

If you're feeling overwhelmed right now, believe me, I understand. I have been there quite a few times before, and it is a rite of passage for any serious organizer. This is especially true in the area of immigration. Xenophobia has been a rationalized part of everyday life in this country for years, with immigrants serving as convenient scapegoats for the failures of neoliberal politics.

Yes, this is scary. No, we are not lost, and we are far from vanquished. Here are some suggestions that I hope may help you on your journey.

This may seem counterintuitive, but the first thing I would say is, don't ignore your need to mourn. The great labor leader Mother Jones famously said: "Don't mourn, organize." I would respectfully like to alter this saying to: "Mourn, then organize." They don't want you to, because mourning requires memory, and fascist politics are about erasing history to point toward a utopia (literally a "no man's land") that will never materialize. You need to ground yourself in the reality of the losses you feel (witnessing families being separated, parents incarcerated, and more). Appreciation for the value of what is lost can be fuel for future battles.

Taking the time out to mourn and reflect can also be a springboard for deeper analysis. This insight became clear to me around the end of the 2000s, during the Obama administration. When I started to do anti-deportation work with the Detention Task Force, I saw family after family being separated. One story radicalized me. We had been fighting the deportation of a man, a farmworker, who had been in the country for many years, did not have a criminal record, and had a US citizen wife and two US citizen children who were clearly traumatized by the prospect of having to lose their father. After a two-year struggle, the man decided that he'd had enough of the fight and was taking voluntary departure: he agreed to self-deport. I remember sitting in a church and crying. I kept going over it in my head: Could I have done more? Sent out more petitions? Written more letters to judges? Arranged more media interviews? Contacted more elected representatives? But then I realized something that has stayed with me for years: this is not about fairness, nor is it about my individual efforts. This is about a cold, brutal machine of a system that I needed to understand at a granular level. I realized that the immigration fight was a subset of the larger fight against the prison industrial complex. Pausing to attend to my grief was hard, but that pause allowed me to deepen my understanding of the brutal mechanics of the system.

My second suggestion is that you use this moment of crisis to clarify what you are truly fighting for. Are you simply about reforming the system, or are you about transformation? Both are hard, but transformation takes much longer. I have come to believe over the years that the US immigration system cannot simply be rejiggered; it must be radically altered into something that respects migrants' human right to live, love, and work where they please in an increasingly globalized society. Because of the scope of the mission, this is not likely to be achieved through mere congressional wrangling.

This became clear to me when I got involved in organizing struggles centered around the passage of Deferred Action for Childhood Arrivals (DACA) and some version of "immigration reform." There, I first noticed a mechanism I have come to call "the cycle." It goes like this: Immigrants and their accomplices come to Democratic legislators and propose an idea. Dem legislators tell us: "That is not a good idea; it is too disruptive and un-strategic." Immigrants decide to do the action anyway (see: the DREAM 9, prison infiltrations, shutting down streets, sit-ins, etc...). It works and moves the conversation forward. Once the success of those actions is apparent, Democratic Party legislators co-opt it and claim that it was theirs in the first place. Then the cycle repeats, going back to the first step. Every win we have obtained as a community has involved the uphill battle of convincing Democratic Party leadership first. But even achieving DACA was a long struggle, and by the time we got to the last serious attempt at immigration reform in 2013, it became apparent that the legislation that we had fought so hard to achieve was deeply inadequate to the crisis. Though it is often talked about as a great lost opportunity in the movement, that legislation had grown so conservative in scope (a twelve-to-fifteen-year path to citizenship, tying status to work requirements, and so on) that even the prison industry considered endorsing it, betting on the fact that it would lead to so much incarceration that they would ultimately benefit. It occurred to me then how much time and effort we had spent as organizers only to get to legislative "solutions" that were deeply inadequate to the liberation of undocumented people. From that point on, my north star became the utter transformation of the system. However, that meant accepting that I was in an intergenerational struggle and that I may not live to see my goals realized.

As always: don't panic. Take stock instead. Where was the movement twenty years ago? Where could the movement be twenty years from today? Pushing for the human right of migrants to live, love, and work where we please is a radical proposition in this historical moment. It might take a lifetime or more to achieve. Be anchored in the fact that many of the rights we take for granted (some of which are once again at risk) were both deeply unpopular at first and took multiple generations to win. We study the points in history when things change, but we often ignore the many years a movement spends in the political wilderness. I've been organizing on immigration for a little over twenty years, and I realize that that is a small fraction of the overall length of a movement. From an organizing point of view, I've literally just gotten started. This is not to discourage you in terms of the effort ahead; this is about grounding you in the understanding that history moves very, very slowly. You are here to do your part, not to know what the timeline of the work looks like.

Conduct an honest appraisal of the work you have already done. Allow yourself to feel grateful for the wins you have achieved but also take a ruthless inventory of what has worked and what hasn't. Search your brain for any dogmas you may have created over the years that may need to be discarded in light of new information.

Moments of crisis are great for strategic reorganizing. I remember a moment in the early 2010s when I was doing local work on immigration in Syracuse. A lot of allies had started to turn away from the immigration fight. It was getting harder and harder to recruit volunteers. Instead of staying stuck in what felt like irrelevance and stagnation, the local group I worked with, the Alliance of Communities Transforming Syracuse (ACTS), engaged in intentional, agenda-free conversations with local African American and Latinx leaders to hear what they were working on. What emerged from that dialogue was an understanding that the issue of racial profiling was one of high concern, and since many of the immigrants with whom we were advocating were being targeted by Immigration and Customs Enforcement (ICE) and CBP as a result of being stopped by police, we aligned ourselves with these African American and Latinx leaders and pushed for (and eventually won) a police command order that would prohibit local law enforcement from asking drivers questions about their national origin during routine traffic stops. This successful campaign created the relationships that eventually, two or three years later, allowed us to convince local officials to make Syracuse a sanctuary city. Crises are hard, but they also present opportunities to think creatively about how to engage the public more effectively. Sometimes, it is worth checking in on people in other movements to find strategic points in common that you can work on together.

Ask yourself who your true allies have been—the folks who have been steadfast through the good and bad times. Identifying these individuals is crucial. Indeed, very few things are more valuable to an activist than an accomplice who has shown up consistently in organizing battles. Those allies can come from surprising places. When my work focused on farmworkers in Central New York, there were occasions where some farm owners were surprisingly willing to help fight for their own workers' rights.

We are not powerless. The fascists are in power, but they have not won. The future is yet to be determined. What you are facing is what every generation of changemakers has faced: a deeply reactionary period. I'm not trying to minimize the losses. But the present moment is not the future. Do not let despair take hold. The future is the future, and it is yet to be determined.

This country was built on genocide and the exploitation of Native, migrant, and slave labor, and that foundation is still felt now. Forget this at your own peril: to do so would be to minimize the scope of the work needed to repair the damage. Anchor your analysis in the knowledge that you are a part of an intergenerational struggle that has had its natural ebbs and flows. Call on your ancestors, especially the ones who have fought battles equal to or worse than the one you are facing now.

Do not let your resentment of citizens' acquiescence to this sordid state of affairs lead you to a politics of bitterness and despair. The reason for the popularity of this toxic politics is that many citizens themselves have also lost out economically over the past thirty to forty years. Grow your analysis and compassion instead of reducing it. Your job is to care, even for the voters who chose to vote for fascism. It is not easy to remember, but your fate is also tied to them. Your overall goal is to reduce the amount of suffering you see, regardless of who the victim is. The right delights in offering voters targets of aggression. The left is about lifting all boats. We have the healthier answers. Have faith in that. Faith in your community.

At the base of all of this must be a trust in the grassroots and in the genius of everyday people. This is the real jewel of organizing: that it is rooted in a belief that the community already has the wisdom to come up with healthy solutions to deep societal problems. It's just that our political structures make it hard for that community to reach those conclusions, and one of your roles as an organizer is to change those structures and make it easier for people to express the goodness in their hearts.

This was never meant to be easy. All of the organizers I know and love have gone through hard times when there is temptation to despair and had to learn to push through. But these challenging times can also be the moments you plant seeds that will bear future fruit. Plant those seeds in joy, grief, and whatever other emotion you may be going through. Be as gentle with yourself as you are hard on those oppressive systems. Remember that you are rooted in the work of those who came before you and are preparing a way for those who will come after. Simply do your part.

Sincerely,
Aly

Aly Wane is an undocumented human rights organizer originally from Senegal, currently living in Syracuse, New York. He is a member of the Syracuse Peace Council and the advisory boards of the Immigrant Justice Network and Freedom University.

Read This if You Are Struggling with Grief

Tanuja Devi Jagernauth

Dear Friend,

    However you arrive at this letter, please know that you are not alone. As of this writing at the end of 2024, our communities are grieving four more years of a Donald J. Trump administration, over a year of US-backed assault on Palestine and (more recently) Lebanon, the loss of trust in so many people and institutions, the loss of political homes, and the loss of loved ones.

    As you navigate this time of great loss, I will offer you reflections from a grief-laden near decade of my life when I experienced a spectrum of losses, from the closure of a beloved project to the death of loved ones. I've been on a few front lines of grief, and I want to offer you something to tuck away for times when even reaching for a letter like this feels impossible.

    Before I jump into my story, I want to place all of this within a larger frame of love. As you grieve, I want to invite you to keep in mind that the grief you're experiencing is a reflection of your capacity for love and the awareness that each of our lives is precious.

    Chances are that love, grief, and loss are what brought you to organizing in the first place, and that you have been organizing and fighting as a way of coping with grief. Mourning the loss of a loved one to the police or the prison system, you may have joined others to begin the work of fighting police brutality and the prison industrial complex. Mourning the loss of resources and safety in our medical system, you may have taken on the work of healing justice, fighting the medical industrial complex, ableism, electeds in office, oppressive social services, and the generational trauma they perpetuate in our communities. You may be a student fighting for justice in a corrupt academic institution. Your work toward a more liberated world may happen across multiple struggles, and chances are it's all rooted in a deep love for yourself, your communities, and those who will be entering the spaces we leave behind after we are gone.

While painful, inconvenient, and at times even shocking in the way it manifests, our grief assures us that we are alive and that our ability to care is intact. If you have any room to hold this recognition, and even celebrate it, I want to pause and invite you to do so.

One place where three comrades and I did our best to practice and promote self- and community care was Sage Community Health Collective. Sage was a nonhierarchical, worker-owned wellness center we cofounded in 2011. We believed in challenging systemic health disparities and the traditional patient/practitioner dynamic by providing affordable, accessible, trauma-informed, and harm reductionist healing services. We primarily offered individual and community acupuncture, bodywork, and herbal/nutritional guidance to our clients. We offered workshops, skillshares, drop-in ear acupuncture, and monthly Community Care Nights in partnership with community members, politicized healers, and freedom fighters. We operated for close to five years.

We knew that we could not completely eliminate the power differential between a patient and a practitioner, but there were things we could do to help patients have as much agency and self-determination when they worked with us, from the time they entered our door to the time they left. We practiced harm reduction by giving our patients a chance to engage and consent at every part of the process in a variety of ways, and especially when discussing herbal, nutritional, or lifestyle changes, which in the dominant culture can so easily be prescriptive or demand abstinence. We worked with patients to help them identify sources of harm in their own lives and strategized with them around what they wanted to change. We were aware that despite our best intentions, our impact could inevitably be harmful to someone, especially during bodywork or acupuncture.

We worked with trusted advisors to create a grievance policy and process that was printed out and shared in English and Spanish in all of our treatment rooms and common areas. In the grievance policy, we broke down how we define harm, how we prevent it, options for intervening when harm occurs, and options for transforming the conditions that enabled the harm to happen in the first place. Among the practitioners, we had group agreements about how we would treat one another, and we created a mutual-agreement form that detailed the ways in which practitioners and patients would work with each other.

We did beautiful work with and for our beloved communities. At the same time, our structure had some serious gaps when it came to taking care of and preventing harm for the cofounders of the collective. As a small business that was also a worker-owned collective, Sage was structured such that all income was first applied to paying our office rent and bills. Whatever was left over was distributed equally among the four collective members once per month. No one's take-home pay reflected the hours they put into the work they did at Sage, our monthly income was not a living wage for any of us, we received no traditional workplace benefits, and we did not structure the organization to guarantee any sick time or paid time off. For a small business, time off is income loss.

One year after we opened, one of our collective members decided to leave. Today, I completely understand why, but at the time it was devastating, to say the least. As a "good immigrant" and someone who had experience in running a private practice, I swallowed my grief, put my head down, and did what I needed to do to keep the business moving.

In our second year, a second collective member left, and again we did not stop. Two of us kept the business running until the other co-owner and I decided to transition her role at Sage. Instead of being a co-owner, she would function more like a renter in the space.

By 2015, four years after we opened, I was running Sage alone. In a word, I was tired. Then, that July, I got some of the worst news of my life. One of my best friends of fourteen years had stage-four breast cancer and would be discontinuing her treatments. I was devastated again. And again, I felt that I could not stop working. I could not reduce my hours. I could not accompany my friend in these last months of her life in the way that I wanted to. I had to keep the business running. This time, however, I would not be able to simply continue business as usual. Something big finally cracked inside of me. I felt the crushing reality that life is very short and that for some, like my dear friend, it can be cut short against your will and all your best efforts.

I realized I could not continue living as I had been, working six or seven days per week with very little pay and very little life outside of Sage. I had to admit that I was not actually living my values, and, most painfully, I felt that I had unwittingly become an absent friend, partner, and community member through overwork and sheer lack of free time. I realized that I had become tired of creating a beautiful community in which I could not fully participate, and that my own personal goals had become stymied as I worked to support others in achieving theirs.

Perhaps in a manifestation of my deep exhaustion and flight stress response, I felt that I no longer wanted to live in a Chicago without my friend. She had been my first roommate and had witnessed my entire life there—the good, the bad, the ugly. I felt that I had to leave and start focusing on my creative pursuits, and all of that meant closing Sage. I decided I would close up shop the following year, in order to give everyone working there as much time as possible to transition to other spaces.

I supported my friend with acupuncture when she was able to come to our space, and I did as many home visits for her as I could. On a Tuesday in November, she passed away at home with her family by her side. I took a few days off, but as the sole owner and operator of the space, I still had to keep the business open and running.

Looking back, I wish I had given myself shorter workdays, fewer workdays, or just pressed pause on the work altogether so that I could be with my dying friend and my grief. I wish I had cultivated a practice of being honest and vulnerable about my needs and feelings. I wish I had worked to develop trust in the people around me to ask for relief from some of my normal duties before, during, and after Sage was closed. I wish I had enlisted friends, patients, comrades, or even friendly acquaintances to help me craft and send a time-off letter and activate a fundraiser for the time off. I could have asked others to handle the admin while I rested, grieved, and spent time with my friend.

Once Sage was officially closed, thanks to capitalism, I had to immediately begin seeking new gigs to pay the bills. What I needed was at least a month off all work to rest, to cry, and to sit with the immense loss of this project and the community we had created in our space. I needed regular accompaniment and a regular place to go where I could face the loss and be with all of it in the company of supportive people. I needed this support to truly grieve, return to myself, and choose how I wanted to move forward with life.

As I write this letter to you, I have to wonder what harm reduction could have looked like before I had my epiphany moment in July 2015, when I was forced to confront crisis. What would it have been like if our practice of harm reduction had applied to collective members as much as it did to the patients we served? In the absence of this time and space for rest, I kept it moving, finding ways to grieve however I could. I took up pottery. Clay became my witness and mirror. I took on an unpaid internship at a new play development center in Chicago. Playwriting became an outlet and a way to envision new worlds beyond my pain. I found deep joy and catharsis in the act of playwriting, and yet, similarly to when I was an acupuncturist, as a low-paid arts administrator and freelance dramaturg, I found myself broke and burning the candle at both ends just to pay the bills.

For the next few years, my untended grief and emotions led me to make some questionable choices and more self-isolation. I coped with the overwhelming whiteness and experiences of harassment I faced in theater by drinking more than usual. I continued to fill my hours with work, commuting, and writing late into the night. Even though on some level I knew better, I avoided my feelings and neglected my body. I eventually paid for this gap in my practice with the loss of a dear friend—not to death this time but to unacknowledged, unaddressed, and untransformed conflict.

I was unable to truly stop, rest, and reckon with myself until 2020, when the entire world also had to stop and reckon with the COVID-19 pandemic and the colossal losses that we began to collectively witness for years. In the wake of Breonna Taylor's and George Floyd's murders, organizers, activists, and educators urged us all to do more to excavate the roots of white supremacy. Tema Okun's work on white supremacy culture characteristics and its antidotes circulated heavily among my networks at this time.

When I read Okun's article, a dozen light bulbs and alarm bells went off in my mind. In the list of white supremacy culture characteristics, I saw so much of my experience running Sage and so much of my behavior as a theatermaker reflected back at me. It became crystal clear to me that I had a lot of unlearning and relearning to do if I wanted to truly help dismantle anti-Blackness in the spaces I occupy and create. In 2020, I memorized each characteristic and its antidote as I began a new job at an all-POC environmental justice organization. I worked hard to practice as many of the antidotes as I could on a daily basis, and I made an effort to catch and counter the white supremacy characteristics when they showed up in my own behavior. I had no idea the antidotes would help me and my family navigate several harrowing months to come.

In March of 2021, I got the kind of phone call that I had dreaded since I moved to Chicago. My dad—master gardener, educator, artist, and my first political comrade—had been admitted to the hospital. They had found a tumor in his brain. The seizures, speech, and vision issues that he had been having were not due to a questionable diagnosis of "epilepsy" but a stage-four glioblastoma in the temporal lobe of his brain. I dropped everything and flew home to Peoria, Arizona, where my family lived and I had grown up. I ended up staying for six months. My family supported my dad through chemo, radiation, and his devastatingly swift decline.

By then, thankfully, I was going to therapy on a weekly basis. To the best of my compromised ability, I embraced imperfection and countered it with a focus on what I was grateful for each day. I checked myself as much as I could when I felt aggression, urgency, and binary thinking rearing their heads. Thankfully, I had found my way to a new job that allowed me to adjust my work hours and workload to accommodate the schedule of appointments and care for my dad. Keeping my workload realistic during this time was a true game changer.

At home, I put all of my facilitation, de-escalation, organizing, grounding, and wellness tools to work, adapting the antidotes to white supremacy culture to create a flexible, shared decision-making process with my grieving, under-slept family.

During this harrowing time, my family and I were able to experience joy, albeit reluctantly. We celebrated my and my brother's birthdays. When we were not taking care of my dad, we passed the time in the evenings at my parents' house playing board games, watching playoff basketball, and playing badminton in the backyard, my dad's pride and joy, where he had installed the irrigation system, laid down the rocks, planted every tree and bush, and seeded and meticulously maintained the lawn, in spite of Arizona's desert heat.

As uncomfortable as it was, I shared what was going on with trusted friends and comrades. When they offered help, I accepted it. I pressed pause on the handful of organizing and mutual aid projects I had initiated the previous year, and I did my best to allow myself the full range of my emotions. I joined a support group for families of cancer patients, expanding the web of care to which I had access. I rested when I needed to rest. I cried when I needed to cry.

Friends surprised me by showing up in the ways they could. They sent me care packages, memes, and check-in texts. They processed medical industrial complex and family shenanigans on the phone with me. One friend sent my family a giant box of assorted pints of ice cream; another sent a strawberry-covered cheesecake. Together we got through what could have been deeply traumatic in the absence of so much community support. By the time my dad died in July, I had a network of support that would get me through the roughest periods of my grief and the creation of a new normal without him in my life.

In this time of so much loss, you may be feeling a wide range of emotions. You may be feeling empty and numb. You might not be sleeping very well. You might be feeling drained. Conversely, you might be full of restless energy, and it might feel hard to sit still. Your mind might be racing. You might not be eating well or hydrating adequately. You might not feel like you have the motivation to take care of yourself in the ways you normally do.

You may have a robust network of support at the ready, just waiting for you to activate it. You may not.

However you are feeling and experiencing this moment, I want you to know that you get to do your grief in your own way.

I certainly questioned the validity of my grief around closing Sage. Feeling undone by the end of a project that I chose to close didn't seem right. Sage wasn't a person. But in closing Sage, I not only lost people who were dear to me; I lost a dream, the thing that I had worked so hard to create with my comrades. Sage had been my answer to so many inequities in the medical industrial complex and beyond, the thing that gave me a sense of place and belonging in movement work, and the way I was able to demonstrate love for my comrades. If you find yourself grieving the end of a project like this, I want to say that not only do you have every right to grieve, but it is within your grief that the seeds of your next era may dwell.

Don't make the mistakes I made in avoiding my grief. I invite you to get to know yours. Become intimate with it.

As you would with anyone new to your life or to your organization, consider having a one-on-one with your grief. Sit down with it, meet it someplace casual, someplace cozy where you can get a drink and a snack. If you prefer, knock on its door and have a chat in its living room. However you desire, I invite you to get to know your grief: what tends to call it forth, where it tends to show up in your body, its colors, its textures.

You need not have an agenda or goal as you befriend your grief. In the same way that healing has no timeline, in the same way that real friendships develop at their own pace, this process of becoming intimate with your grief will not be linear. Give it time. Listen and watch as the love at the core of your grief eventually emerges.

If fear rises up and chills your spine, I invite you to notice it and reach for a practice that helps you to find safety and even pleasure in your body. If perfectionism clenches your jaw and drives you toward urgency, aggression, binary thinking, and rigidity, I invite you to notice it as kindly as you can, pause, and take a deep breath. Grief is messy, and it's always okay to make mistakes. Whatever you are trying to do right now can be achieved in so many different ways, and I invite you to give it all the time it needs. Release any unrealistic expectations that you might be holding over your own head. Center your own rest and healing as much as humanly possible, and when you feel like denying and hiding your pain and isolating, this is when I really need you to pause. This path will only worsen.

In order to embrace your grief, you may need to put down some of the work you are currently doing and ask for support from those around you.

Asking for support can feel really tough, even if you have been here before; even if you have supported others through grief before. For some of us, accepting support may go against everything we have been taught in this hyper-individualistic economic structure, obsessed as it is with self-sufficiency and self-reliance. Consider this a moment to practice pushing back against the dominant white supremacist culture. By embracing an opportunity to receive care and support, you are helping us all create a world rooted in truly reciprocal relationships. I can finally say from experience: asking for support, receiving it, and taking the time and space you need to heal can be a profound act of harm prevention in the long run.

As a fellow isolator with an extra-spicy exile narrative (thanks colonialism and generational trauma!) I want you to know: the voice telling you that no one wants or needs to hear your pain—the voice telling you that no one can handle your pain—is completely full of shit. I encourage you to find a support group, call a hotline or warmline that you trust, reach out to a therapist if you can access one, and, if you have supportive friends and family around you, let them support you.

This can take so many different forms, and if this form of sharing power is new to you, consider starting with something small, and celebrate every time you let someone in. Let someone bring you food or send you a gift card for groceries or food delivery. Let folks know that you are open to receiving care packages, and let them surprise you with what they send. If you take walks alone, maybe invite a friend or two to accompany you in silence, or however you need.

You may be wondering how on earth you will be able to receive so much care when you are not able to give anyone a single damn thing right now. You may be wondering how you deserve any of this support. You may be wondering what you will have to do to repay everyone around you who is helping you get through this time. If so, I totally get it. If I may, I would love to offer a reframe and an invitation.

Racial capitalism and white supremacy culture have us living very isolated and individualistic lives. Many of our institutions are held together through transactional relationships that often replicate carceral logics and systems of oppression. I invite you to take this opportunity to experiment with what reciprocal relationships might be able to look like.

In the world so many of us are trying to build, our relationships are not extractive or built upon an expectation of immediate material reward attached to every action. Our relationships are reciprocal, generative, fluid, organic, spacious, filled with life, and rooted in love. We are living bell hooks's vision for loving relationships by extending ourselves to one another in the spirit of nurturing each other's holistic, spiritual growth. You have the opportunity to help create this world by rehearsing it right now, in this time of grief.

I invite you to let others extend themselves to you in this time, and I invite you to practice vulnerability by just receiving right now. You did not have to do a thing to deserve this support, and when you have moved through this moment, you do not owe anyone anything beyond what we all owe to each other through our relational bonds.

Try to receive support with grace and gratitude, and continue to focus on your healing process. If anything, a you that is alive, as well as possible, and able to participate in a reciprocal relationship with someone can be the gift you "give back" to that person, your loved ones, and the world we are trying to cocreate.

Everything we love will end one day. Everyone we love will pass. Staying alive and aging, then, becomes a complicated privilege. As we continue to live and love, the things we mourn will multiply. Inside of the excruciating pain you feel right now is life, love, and a precious, broken, yet still-beating mosaic heart. Cherish, protect, and honor it.

There was a time in my life when I know I would have said something about "not having the luxury to grieve." Today I would counter that haughty, hurting, and avoidant self by saying, "If you don't have the luxury to grieve, then you don't have the luxury to love." I don't know what sort of loveless movement I was trying to build back then, but I am grateful to be committed to a different practice with value-aligned comrades today.

Never be afraid or ashamed to grieve, as it is an expression of your love. Grief is and will always be a reflection of our capacity to love, and it is our grief that will keep us human in these times as fascism attempts to grow where solidarity belongs.

We must let our humanity bring us together instead of tearing us apart. We must allow our grief to help turn us toward each other and be the glue that binds us together. If that which we mourn must multiply, let it make us unstoppable.

I continue to learn how to grieve and embrace my deep and abiding love for our movements. I continue to unlearn the habits of dominant culture. I continue to do my best to practice community in the face of my own isolationist tendencies. I continue to grieve for Sage and the community I had while it was functioning. I continue to grieve for my dear friend and my dad. As I grieve, I try to do better. I try to avoid making the mistakes of the past, and I do my best to honor the lives of my departed loved ones by living as fully and with as much joy as I can.

From my own broken, yet still-beating mosaic heart to yours, this is the work of my lifetime, and it might be yours too. Please know that you are held and seen with love—and you are never, ever alone.

In loving solidarity,
Tanuja

Tanuja Devi Jagernauth is an Indo-Caribbean immigrant, writer, theatermaker, and liberatory yoga educator committed to advancing the abolition of the prison industrial complex from a creative and healing justice lens. She lives with her partner and dog in Chicago, Illinois.

Conclusion
Read This if You're Wounded and Want to Quit

Kelly Hayes

Dear Friend,

    At some point in all of our movement journeys, we experience a fracture—a loss so severe, it feels like we've been cut open and something has been snatched from within us. It may be the loss of a group or organization that has come undone due to conflict, upheaval, or repression, or whose members have rejected us. It may be the loss of a friend we have marched with and schemed with, or even endured the blows of police alongside. I am not talking about death but about schisms, when people and entities we loved and for whom we sacrificed simply aren't ours anymore. It's a kind of breakup, and we all know how emotionally painful the end of loving relationships can be. In my experience, the loss of friendship, of comradery, of the work of place making—where we endeavored to understand what freedom was and could be together—can be more traumatic than the collapse of a romantic relationship.

    Sometimes these moments, when groups and relationships fall apart, are so painful that activists give up on organizing, or the ideas that brought them into movements. When organizations, groups, campaigns, and friendships fall apart, we can feel undone. I want to talk about how I've healed from such moments, and how we can find our way back to the work of making change.

    For me, movements are home. They are where I grew up, not in a physical sense but in terms of actual maturation, and becoming the person I would be. My childhood involved some exposure to activism through my mother, who was an advocate for public education. I was also politically active in my twenties. When I was in my late-twenties and early-thirties, I learned the craft of organizing, and that process was transformational for me. A friend I met during that era once joked that we grew up together in our thirties, and she was completely right. I was in my thirties when I received the mentorship I needed to overcome my emotional immaturity, and to unlearn survival mechanisms that had led me to reenact old conflicts and reactions, rather than learning and responding and growing with people. It was then that I learned the skills I needed to work across difference and prioritize connection and collective survival over comfort and easy agreement. This was an imperfect, stumbling process, but it was a transformative one. I would not be the person I am without the mentors, friends, and co-strugglers I knew then, or the skills they helped me develop.

When I think about my feelings about that time, I think about the poem, "Relating to the Origin," by my friend Atena Danner. She writes:

> I know this song
> I belong here.
> Let me tell you how I got here.
>
> Movement was my government cheese,
> my block on Damon Street in Flint, Michigan at sunset.
> Activism was my immunization, my after-school program,
>   my family.

I say I grew up in movements because I became myself in movements. I have also lost more than I can possibly account for here over the course of my organizing work.

Sometimes loss comes in the form of defeat. When I was part of the Mental Health Movement—an effort to save Chicago's publicly funded mental healthcare clinics—I had friends and co-strugglers who swore they would die if they lost their clinics, and some of them did. We lost the campaign, we lost the clinics we were fighting for, and we lost our friends. (Though it's worth noting that, today, some of those clinics are being restored, after years of organizing: even our defeats are part of a profound lineage that can help shift the course of history.) Such losses generally occur because the forces we are up against are powerful, and too often, the systems that would exploit and dispose of us succeed in their death-making work. Sometimes, however, we experience loss because siblings in struggle cease to understand each other, furiously disagree, or even come to despise one another.

Trying to maintain relationships under the strain of intense movement work can be difficult. Sometimes, the ties that bind us begin to fray before we even notice. Once, when a friendship I cherished fell apart, it seemed to happen suddenly. My friend became angry about something I said, and overnight, our bond was broken. I couldn't fathom how this rift could become so absolute so quickly, but in truth, it had probably been forming for a long time, in ways I had failed to notice. Overwhelmed by my obligations, I simply didn't recognize that the relationship was unraveling.

As organizers, many of us are exhausted by dueling obligations. In "Relating to the Origin," Atena captures that head-spinning disorientation:

> I am scrolling on social media, unable to stop.
> I am trapped, horror-struck between the lenses of endlessly streaming eyes.
> I am running down State Street toward the gathering crowd, surprising myself with a guttural howl,
> I am working two jobs, working three jobs,
> trying to show up. When I can: show up;
> Drinking rocket fuel, eating lightning so I can show the fuck up.

Juggling the demands of capitalism, the needs of our loved ones, and the work of movements can be overwhelming. We can become dysregulated, heavily activated, prone to conflict. We can become confused about when it's time to ask questions and when it's time to fight. We may assume too much about what other people want or believe, or where they're coming from. We may reenact old patterns tied to old traumas that have nothing to do with the moment at hand. Or, we can find ourselves on the receiving end of these behaviors. In the worst case, we can become part of a dynamic where everyone involved is projecting, assuming, and acting defensively, creating a continuum of hurt, angst, and harm that expands to fill any space we occupy together.

Sometimes we lack the tools we need to address these dynamics before they unravel groups and relationships. Sometimes people are not interested in mediation or difficult conversations, because they are steeped in their convictions about what's right and what should happen next. Sometimes people have changed, or perhaps revealed their true character, and they are not people we can trust or build with any longer. However it happens, sometimes what binds us is undone, and our connections are severed.

Starting over from this position can lead us to question everything. A friend whose group came undone once told me she felt like she had failed at the most important thing in her life. I think a lot of activists who have experienced the collapse of their movement home can identify with that feeling. In my own work, I have experienced the loss of groups, communities, and relationships that had shaped my life. I have been left utterly heartsick, unable to imagine how I would reconstitute my efforts, and unsure I even wanted to.

In fact, there was a time when I was convinced I wanted out. I even tried to walk away. I was embittered. People I trusted had let me down, and if I'm honest, I felt humanity itself had let me down. Amid the repression of activists, and the broader society's indifference to war—which had become background noise in this country—and the normalization of so much cruelty and violence, I had little hope for the future. My community was in disarray. Our belief in each other, which had always persisted during the hard times, had seemingly evaporated.

I can remember thinking, "Good luck, humanity," as I turned my attention to myself and focused on repairing my own life—a life that had fallen apart, in many ways, while I devoted myself to political matters.

During my temporary breakup with social change, I worked on myself. I did things I should have been doing all along, like getting therapy and medical care, and expressing myself artistically. I took up photography, which wound up being critically important to my emotional recovery. Taking photos, as a hobby, meant that I could wander around Chicago, whenever I had time, and become fascinated with a puddle, a leaf, or some glitter on the sidewalk. I could focus on trying to capture what was special about anything around me that struck me as beautiful, and in so doing, I slowly fell in love with the world again.

My bitterness began to recede. It was as though my bones had been broken and were knitting back together. Like a person who swears they'll never love again, after a horrific breakup, I had sworn off fighting for the world with which I was again becoming enamored, and sworn off fighting for other people, but that rigidity was beginning to ease.

Eventually, old friends began to reach out. The Occupy movement was kicking off nationwide, and there was a hub in our city. "Come down here, you have to see this," they would say.

I brushed off these invitations, saying I wasn't interested in protest. But I was interested. I was simply unwilling. I was protecting myself. I was resisting the possibility of being hurt again. I was resisting the possibility of losing myself again.

"We need you down here," my friend said.

I declined, again and again. Until, one day, I didn't. I saw something on social media that made me angry—an act of abuse against a crowd, the kind of indignity that protesters so often experience—and I got on a train. I headed downtown.

When I joined the fray, I felt like I was stepping back into myself, back into hope, back into possibility. As Atena writes:

> Unprepared, but ready
> Halting, but forward—
> I know this song.
>
> Bucket drum beat, orange lights,
> I am lying on the ground, singing

My journey in movements began again. That journey would transform me as a person. It would make anything good and meaningful I've done in the intervening years possible. It would bring people, groups, and formations into my life that would be as dear to me as family. But those connections were sometimes broken, and feelings of disappointment, loss, betrayal, and heartbreak are still part of my experience. These things never go away. They are part of being alive, and in movements, we live life intensely. We are intentionally aware of suffering that others phase out, to live more comfortably within a false peace. We fight for each other, build things together, defend each other, de-arrest each other, and make commitments to something much larger than ourselves. We are bound by intentions we hold sacred. When our efforts and our relationships fracture, the pain is excruciating because of the profundity of the lives we are living together.

As Atena puts it, "I am dancing into traffic, leaning into faith." Falling from those heights, from that extremity of being, breaks something inside of us that must be allowed to heal.

What does that healing look like? I think the first step is understanding that what you are experiencing, while terrible, is normal. As my friend Dean Spade told me when we discussed these kinds of fractures, "Everyone I know has been through this. I've been through this." Dean emphasized that we all bring emotional baggage into movement spaces that gets unpacked in messy ways. This is true of us, and of our co-strugglers. "We all show up with our stuff, and we play it out. We play out family roles, and we play out prior woundings. We play out things we don't know about ourselves," Dean explained. "It's normal, and it doesn't mean that you are worse or better than anyone else who's trying to do social movement work. Anything we do that betters will include conflict, and it's so painful."

Dean stressed that when fractures happen within groups, we have the opportunity to question the patterns that drove people apart. "We can make space to figure out, what was hard? What could have supported the group to have a different outcome? What, in my behavior or in the group's culture, could have helped?" Dean noted that when we're experiencing a "shame spiral," it's easy to exceptionalize ourselves as especially bad or inept, when really, we're just experiencing something fundamentally human.

Of course, we're not always ready to grapple with those questions right away. We often need time to feel the pain we're in, to make space for the feelings and practice of grief. We probably need to honor what we've lost and its place in our lives, whether that's a relationship or an organization. We need to let ourselves hurt, and let ourselves feel the full range of emotions that accompany our loss, from anger to bewilderment. All of our feelings need to be felt; if we try to subdue them and march on as though nothing happened, they will likely swell up and spill out in other situations, in a manner we cannot control. Make space for your pain, and be gentle with yourself. You're human, and when humans hurt, we need to be held. What makes you feel held? What makes you feel whole? Engage in those activities and experiences.

When you've had time to feel and express raw emotions, you might be ready to reflect and ask the kind of questions Dean raised about what went wrong.

In retrospect, I can recognize that a number of movement environments with which I've been involved were toxic in different ways. Sometimes I contributed to that toxicity. At this stage of my life, I don't revisit these memories with anger, shame, or recrimination. I look to these moments as lessons about how society and trauma shape us, and shape our groups, and how we and our group cultures have the capacity to evolve.

If you have made space for your pain and engaged with difficult questions about what happened, and why, you may still feel pretty raw about your experiences and hesitant to reengage with movement work. That's okay. My best advice at this stage is to engage in activities that ground you in your values and remind you of what you love about the world, or even what you love about other people. Whether that means spending time on a hobby (artistic or otherwise), volunteering, or reconnecting with the earth, give yourself the chance to feel grounded and to appreciate what's sacred to you. If you returned to the fight, what would you be fighting for? Immerse yourself in that. Let it envelop you. Feel that deep love.

Lastly, I encourage you to think about relationships and collaborations that went well. When did the work feel right? When did it give you a sense of purpose? What bonded you to other people in ways that were healthy and life-giving? If you were to return and build a new political home, what would you want it to be like? What's worth rebuilding in a new way? What would you want to reimagine entirely?

Things that fail and fall apart aren't worthless. They're part of us. They're part of history. They're part of a learning process that continually reiterates itself across time and space, as we make and unmake the worlds we inhabit, and as we are made and unmade by each other.

When you are ready, I also want you to know that the work of place making, of dreaming out loud with other people, of struggling against intractable enemies and building what must exist, is still here. It is still home. It is still yours, if you want it. There is room at the table. There is a sign for you to hold. There are people ready to lock arms with you. There are battles that must be waged. There are containers that must be built. There are hopes that can be realized, and your heart, hands, and creativity are both needed and welcome. Sometimes we need to work on ourselves. Sometimes our expectations must change. Sometimes we need space to heal. But when you are ready, remember Atena's words, and let them be your song:

> I belong here
> We belong here
> Wake into this—our story

With love,
Kelly

Relating to the Origin

Atena Danner

I know this song
I belong here.
Let me tell you how I got here.

Movement was my government cheese,
my block on Damon Street in Flint, Michigan at sunset.
Activism was my immunization, my after-school program, my family.

Which is to say: I was a child. Didn't know why I was there or
what was important or
how much it really meant. To me, it simply was.

Mike Brown was the straw that broke my back. So many terrors
before and since but trauma is a time machine. wounds are checkpoints across our timelines.
I am scrolling on social media, unable to stop.
I am trapped, horror-struck between the lenses of endlessly streaming eyes.
I am running down State Street toward the gathering crowd, surprising myself with a guttural howl,
I am working two jobs, working three jobs,
trying to show up. When I can: show up;

Drinking rocket fuel, eating lightning so I can
show the fuck up.

It was the babies and the smalls and the comrades who gathered me
out of my scattershot attempts to "make a difference."
Who pulled me onto
the collective path.
I was born again, wailing at the chaos of new life:
a child among wiser children, stumbling eager through lessons
Tripping over my unlearning
Stepping hesitantly, on shaking legs, nearly paralyzed with the urgency of things...

Unprepared, but ready
Halting, but forward—
I know this song.

Bucket drum beat, orange lights,
I am lying on the ground, singing,

Smell of asphalt, sweat...
We are arms linked in the throng, singing.

Icy wind and watering eyes
We are marching in the street, singing.

Halyard cord striking through the silence
I am laid open before the crowd, singing: come, oh come. . . . We
belong together.
We are strong together

I am dancing into traffic, leaning into faith

I know this song
I remember that night

I found myself singing along
A song of longing and knowing

Some of us were so focused on the sun. We failed to see the moonlight. Some of us were so focused on the moon, we missed the cartography of the stars. Some of us were so busy looking up we had to learn to look to each other. Some of us have been so focused on looking that we will need to learn listening again
learn touching and feeling again
learn smelling and tasting and seeking again

Drive your hands deep as you can into the dirt. You will know it when you find it.
Don't tell me what is not possible
my time and your breath are better spent
Blowing parachutes of dandelion fluff:
Investing in bright, Black futures dotting the landscape

I belong here
We belong here
Wake into this—our story

Acknowledgments

I want to thank everyone who contributed a letter to this book, bringing their experience, heart, and brilliance to this effort. I am deeply grateful to my beloved husband, Charlie, who is my partner in all things, and to my dear friends, who propel me forward each day. These are the people I would be lost without, and they are part of everything I do.

To my collective, Lifted Voices—which sunsetted in 2024—this book would not exist if we had not existed. Andrea Ritchie, Dean Spade, and Tanuja Jagernauth: I would not have found the words I shared in these pages without you. Robyn Maynard and Leanne Betasamosake Simpson, thank you for your friendship, your work, and your endless inspiration. I also want to thank my sister for writing me letters that challenge me and remind me who we are.

I am grateful to Sophia Hussain for their work as a developmental editor. I also want to thank Maya Schenwar and Kimberly Huntress Inskeep for their editorial advice.

Lastly, I want to thank my late father, Michael Hayes, whose lessons I held close as we worked on this book. I hope he would be proud of it.

About the editor

Kelly Hayes is a Menominee author, organizer, movement educator and photographer. They host Truthout's podcast *Movement Memos* and are co-author of the book *Let This Radicalize You*, with Mariame Kaba. Hayes is also the creator of *Organizing My Thoughts*, a weekly newsletter about politics and justice work.

AK PRESS is small, in terms of staff and resources, but we also manage to be one of the world's most productive anarchist publishing houses. We publish close to twenty books every year, and distribute thousands of other titles published by like-minded independent presses and projects from around the globe. We're entirely worker run and democratically managed. We operate without a corporate structure—no boss, no managers, no bullshit.

The **FRIENDS OF AK PRESS** program is a way you can directly contribute to the continued existence of AK Press, and ensure that we're able to keep publishing books like this one! Friends pay $25 a month directly into our publishing account ($30 for Canada, $35 for international), and receive a copy of every book AK Press publishes for the duration of their membership! Friends also receive a discount on anything they order from our website or buy at a table: 50% on AK titles, and 30% on everything else. We have a Friends of AK ebook program as well: $15 a month gets you an electronic copy of every book we publish for the duration of your membership. *You can even sponsor a very discounted membership for someone in prison.*

Email **friendsofak@akpress.org** for more info, or visit the website: **https://www.akpress.org/friends.html**.

There are always great book projects in the works—so sign up now to become a Friend of AK Press, and let the presses roll!